'Perfect serenity to dream and yet you know you're not dreaming — Our beloved Grandchildren.'

LETTER TO GRANDSON JUN
I Found Myself Hiking

WRITTEN BY *Yeh-Yeh Yeo*   ILLUSTRATED BY *Sania Himawan*

World Scientific

NEW JERSEY · LONDON · SINGAPORE · BEIJING · SHANGHAI · HONG KONG · TAIPEI · CHENNAI · TOKYO

Early youth and AdulTeens learn best through nurturing holistic core qualities keyed up by infectious enthusiasm and the finesse of will as shown by the new generation of young teenage medalists at the Olympics'20 and the US Open'21.

Tan Sri Sharifah Hapsah
President, National Council of Women's Organisations
Co-Founder, Permata - UNDP Awardee for Nurturing the Young in Malaysia

---

Grandson Jun ('tua soon' 大孙) is so fortunate to have a grandpa like YY ('Yeh-Yeh' 爷爷; Hanyu Pinyin: yeye), who is enthusiastic in passing on the wisdom to the next generation.

NUS Professor Dr MY Chew PhD (Tsinghua)
Faculty of Arts & Social Sciences

YY's enthusiasm is indeed contagious as evidenced by him thrice winning the prestigious NTU Team Leadership Award. With propriety as a sweet Swede, I just enquired of him, my host at dinner, whether it's true NTU was looking for a provost. I ended up staying eleven years as NTU Provost and thence 3rd President.

Emeritus NTU Professor Bertil Andersson
Trustee, Nobel Foundation

Life's journey, like driving 3,000 miles across America, is all about the drive, climb and self-learning. We set the difficult ones so that we can truly learn and predominate.

Edmund TL Yong, Tiong Bahru-born Founder CEO X-Celerator with two Unicorns like billion-dollar patent-driven PatSnap; and hobby mountaineer with Edmund Hillary as childhood hero

Published by

World Scientific Publishing Co. Pte. Ltd.
5 Toh Tuck Link, Singapore 596224
USA office: 27 Warren Street, Suite 401-402, Hackensack, NJ 07601
UK office: 57 Shelton Street, Covent Garden, London WC2H 9HE

National Library Board, Singapore Cataloguing in Publication Data
Name(s): Yeo, Yeh-Yeh. | Himawan, Sania, illustrator.
Title: Letter to grandson Jun : I found myself hiking /
    written by Yeh-Yeh Yeo ; illustrated by Sania Himawan.
Description: Singapore : World Scientific Publishing Co. Pte. Ltd., [2022]
Identifier(s): ISBN 978-981-12-5519-9 (hardcover) | ISBN 978-981-12-5591-5 (paperback) |
    ISBN 978-981-12-5520-5 (ebook for institutions) |
    ISBN 978-981-12-5521-2 (ebook for individuals)
Subject(s): LCSH: Conduct of life--Juvenile literature. | Values--Juvenile literature. |
    Yeo, Yeh-Yeh--Travel--United States--Juvenile literature. |
    Automobile travel--United States--Juvenile literature.
Classification: DDC 158.1--dc23

British Library Cataloguing-in-Publication Data
A catalogue record for this book is available from the British Library.

Copyright © 2022 by World Scientific Publishing Co. Pte. Ltd.

All rights reserved. This book, or parts thereof, may not be reproduced in any form or by any means, electronic or mechanical, including photocopying, recording or any information storage and retrieval system now known or to be invented, without written permission from the publisher.

For photocopying of material in this volume, please pay a copying fee through the Copyright Clearance Center, Inc., 222 Rosewood Drive, Danvers, MA 01923, USA. In this case permission to photocopy is not required from the publisher.

For any available supplementary material, please visit
https://www.worldscientific.com/worldscibooks/10.1142/12806#t=suppl

Desk Editor: Jiang Yulin

Typeset by Diacritech Technologies Pvt. Ltd.
Chennai - 600106, India

In Spring, Summer especially in the Autumn-Winter of life by the golden pond, let's renew our bonds with our magnificent Grandchildren in the lovely art of letter writing and courtly familial conversations lest Father Time overtakes us and we begin to forget and imbibe in a multi-variate mix of memories and alternative reality.

Contents

Author Bio .... *vii*
Acknowledgements .... *ix*
Preface .... *xi*

Quadrant I
Hiking, Fast and in Fear 1

Quadrant II
Driving, Faster and Farther 23

Quadrant III
Why Faster & Higher? 47

Quadrant IV
Enthusiasm, Faster & Forever 67

Quadrant V
Warp Speed, Fastest & to the Future 91

Quadrant VI
Sweet Conclusion 109

Attachments *117*

Author Bio

Yeh-Yeh Yeo grew up on an old farm at the original Frankel Estate. He was schooled at Singapore Christian Brothers' SABS-SJI; Cambridge MA, USA; & Cambridge, UK market town. He was a lucky village kid to have gone on to participate in assignments on all continents except Africa and Latin America. Upon retirement, he turned to writing firstly the four volumes on Univer-Cities and now this *Letter to Grandson Jun*, in courtly love of his Magnificent Six Grandchildren ~ XJWYKE.

On a road less travelled, driving 3,000 miles across America, YY takes the role of a sleuth seeking, searching and illustrating. His notations have taken him through the sleepy hollows between disciplines in the hope to uncover more understanding of our world, ourselves and for the next generations to aid in solving increasingly more complex problems.

The narrative draws upon clues from a tapestry of connections encompassing geography, history, philosophy, sport and Greek mythology, literature, movies, etc. with YY's personal experiences and enthusiasm. YY nudges all to explore the alluring unbeknownst spaces in between the usual silos of disciplines. His narrative aims to reach the heart of daily challenges which cumulate to lifelong ones if they remain unresolved. His eureka moment ~ 'I found myself (comma) hiking!'

YY's personal in-conversation style of writing, in the mode of a letter, is akin to a private diary of experiences and personal advice shared with young grandson Jun.

YY quotes Professor Chew who kindly opined: "Grandson Jun ('tua soon' 大孙) is so fortunate to have a grandpa like YY ('Yeh-Yeh' 爷爷; Hanyu Pinyin: yeye), who is enthusiastic in passing on the wisdom to the next generation." Professor Dr M.Y. Chew, PhD (Tsinghua), NUS Faculty of Arts & Social Sciences, Singapore

Acknowledgements

To my elder son Kwan and grandson Jun who were my thought co-incubators for this Letter to Grandson Jun and the consensus to add the binary pun, 'I Found Myself Hiking'.

Thanks to my co-riders over the purple plain, more accurately, the impressionists' pastel hues of the Great Plains:

My successful collaborator Artist-Sculptor Chee Kiong in YOG 2010 who wisely recommended his mentee NAFA, Javanese-American graduate Artist-Visualiser Himawan (from New England Keene where *Jumanji* starring Robin Williams was first filmed).

The trinity of WSPC ~ Award winning editor Triena Ong, Regarded Publisher Hong Koon and Rising Yulin.

My beloved Swee Chee who famously said she treats our Magnificent Six Grandchildren, XJWYKE, equally fairly but more so with the youngest, En.

Our three Sons Seng, Kwan and An and their Akela Spouses Amelia, Suwei and Weisze who went through the text with a fine tooth comb to the last syllable of 25,000 words.

The indomitable Soong and Frank in their trusty auto-steeds of engineering, the classic BMW 2002ti and Mustang Cobra.

And a cast of thousands we met on the hikes, treks, the driving and flying in our wanderlust criss-crossing the globe, anchored by the brotherhood of the highway, a 3,000-mile drive on I-80 across the USA.

The longer centennial wave dating back to 1865 ~ Carroll of Alice, Verne of Moonshot (a hundred years earlier to Armstrong's landing on the Moon in1969), James Mason of Massachusetts who first patented the percolator and the ensuing strong wakeup Trucker's coffee'69 that looked like dish water; and fast forward, winning the 150th Anniversary Tanglin Club circa 1865 Golf Tourney 2015.

Through 70 years from first grade, Lock's been a stalwart pal full of enthusiasm from scouting then to still golfing now, till always our tome of focused last hole last putt. And there's Youthful Nephew Zikri (he had asked free-climber Caldwell to autograph his book *The Push* for me) whose zesty enthusiasm turned his redundancy as a roving wildlife photo-journalist into a reborn hip marketeer ginning up Virgin Airlines Quintessential Archie Rose Gin & Tonic Ad Campaign on the subliminal chic inflight taste of Sydney's own.

To the papable 'entheos' of inspirers like Olympian Gold Medalist Swimmer Joseph Schooling and World Badminton Champion Loh Kean Yew – not forgetting Singapore Champs of yore Neo Chwee Kok and Wong Peng Soon, re-born.

The protean Jackalope of the west in the shadows of the Cowboy State of Wyoming embedded deep in my psyche; and the stars that shone upon us from Singapore to continental North America, advisedly the brilliant North Star of inspiration and guiding.

To the magic of the night sky, the inspiring quiet of early dawn and the climate-change hotter days that silently hot-air-ballooned away, I owe ever a rich debt of gratitude to the making of this Letter ~ a Little Feather of 'done it'.

Last but not least, to Professor Frank Rühli, Dean of the Faculty of Medicine, University of Zurich and member of the Zurich Cantonal Parliament whose letter to Young Oskar will cover his journey through evolutionary medicine, the ubiquitous impact of the Spanish Flu and Covid-19 and variants on their New Normal lives and futures.

Preface

Ode to Entheos ~ In Praise of Enthusiasm to Sustain Our Beloved Grandchildren to Live to 100

Girding us with gifted godly psyche
Dilemmas ~ Impossible writ, I'm possible

For in crisis, there's danger and opportunity
Nietzsche's pathology of distance and apogee

Crowd funded my miles ~ I Found Myself, Hiking
Why ~ Nietzsche made Hyperboreans ever climbing

Teacher Chelvan and Mother launched my rocket
Imagineered for Man-Mars and Lady-Venus planets

Savour earth bounding 3,000 miles across America
Big land, big skies, changing Fortuna-persona

Revolutionary Minuteman from Concord to Cheyenne
Like the intrepid myth, Jackalopean

Quintessentially twin-sharing Protean power
Shape-changing, at defining times reappear

How ~ Relent, re-invent ourselves AND save our beloved blue earth
Why ~ Resides not in Big or Small Dipper Stars but our heart and hearth!

NOTE: This is in poesy, a prefaced summary of YY's *Letter to Grandson Jun – I Found Myself, Hiking* as it might have been at Delphi or in sinic philosophy, 'Know thyself, a hundred battles, a hundred victories'. It's not in the stars, as opined by Shakespeare's Caesar nor even the GPS North Star of the Dipper Constellation.

Quadrant I
Hiking, Fast and in Fear

5 April 2020

Dear Jun,

I had originally thought I would write you a four-segment novella logically beginning with a prequel, moving briskly to the main show, and ending with an epic epilogue and sequel. (I learnt about this form of storytelling structure from the *Star Wars* post-production special-effects refinements and re-shoots process at my client's Levesden UK Studios when they were completing the blockbuster *The Phantom Menace*). Time, however, is a silent thief of everyday life, so I took my own advice to fast forward to the sequel à à à that is, where we are right now, since life often unfolds with such speed when meeting the future. This is the genesis of this letter you are reading right now - *I Found Myself Hiking*.

Hiking at 1mph,

trekking **faster** at 3mph

to hiking at the **fastest** pace,

through to driving at (then permitted) **100mph** across America.

But as you know, in *Star Trek* and *Gundam*, the present can also move at warp speed! If you are incredulous, recall the astronaut super-heroes of Apollo 11 who landed on the Moon in July 1969. Then fast forward to the Corona Pandemic 2019 beginnings and its global spread that created Operation Warp Speed in the race for a vaccine.

It behoves us to gird ourselves in breadth, depth and sinews for our own inner spirit to face the unknown (some of which we don't/can't know or that we don't know yet)!

So, hold tight, onward we go!

It all suddenly burst out when I was on a trip with your Dad to visit his preparatory Sherborne School in the 'coloris automnal' of 2017, some

Quadrant I: Illustrations 1-6

Rugby by Sherborne

30 years after he had graduated. He drove the hatchback Mercedes adroitly, as though with deep local knowledge, on the narrow farm roads where country gentlemen sped like F1 aces.

THE HARE & JACKALOPE

We came by an English hare, with whiskers overlapping a mouthful of grass, startled by our headlights. It was like the hybrid Jackalope, a centaur-like half-rabbit half-antelope, that I had imagined seeing in the low-oxygen mile-high Wyoming mountain city of Cheyenne some 50 years earlier! Long forgotten, I thought. But it began to dawn on me that the Jackalope and all its intriguing qualities of being ever-present, without being imposing, is agile, audacious, cheeky, and thoughtful. It manages to evade man's unending expansion of human habitation. All this remained benignly embedded deep in my psyche! Similarly are the adjectives used by Niccolò Machiavelli describing the God of Fortune as a woman who loves the changing irreverence of younger men because they take risks, sometimes with sweet strength (as in your video games) and who with righteous audacity dare to challenge and command her! But that is only half of the equation. It hides the other half of individual initiative – hard, creative, nimble, intuitive, and beguiling ways to understand people so they will enthusiastically favour you and follow your lead. Intriguing, because I can't seem to shake-off Jackalope and its seductive effervescent fountain of alternate ways, always!

The reality, as it unfolded, was that your Dad has touches of *'Jackalopean'* qualities! As a 12-year old transplanted in the UK some 6,600 miles away from home in Singapore he enjoyed Sherborne a lot more than I had worried about all these past years. He now recalls with some glee getting his classmates out of The Moors (made famous through Sherlock Holmes in the dreadful case of *The Hounds of Baskerville*) on one of his early school cadets' field outings. He was then a rookie from then little known Singapore. He enjoyed playing Under-14 rugby (a ruffian's game played by gentlemen) at Clifton Public (aka Private) School with oversized lads and the inter-school championships at Twickenham. Lo, his eyes lit up when noticing his own younger tinker-schoolboy-self and his Lyon House Head-Boy and mate Trevor Evershed in the photo-pantheon of memories. Trevor was the Rugger captain and is now a home renovator-investor in St Albans where we were to visit later during the trip. It's like zipping from the past and back to the future, like some form of *pas-ture* or more meaningfully, *armature* (the evolving future that's built up from the past and morphing into sometimes unexpected new spaces, uses or lives).

The narrative versus the reality is always with us. And I wanted to tell it as it is. Authentic (no bluffing) with a touch of humour rather than being compelling in what I hope will inspire you and where you may have inspired others, too.

Quadrant I: Illustrations 7-9

Into Jackalope's Famed Gold Cariso Lode Shaft

Lo! The reality set in. It includes an upside-down effect. I realised that your Dad and you have inspired me in what you both have done at a young age! Now how do I make sense of this realisation? My early life was more basic with fewer resources and tech. Yet our dear Singapore raised itself by its bootstraps from Third World to First World led by our Founding Prime Minister Lee Kuan Yew. It dawned on me that I was always enthusiastic even in Primary One. I was the only one to volunteer (others were nominated by the teacher) to take part in our first-ever 'sports day' and a novel 25-yard Lighted Candle Race. Simple rule – first past-the-post with a lighted candle wins. I won!

How, how? The farm-lad enthused and thought forward – be the first to have your candle lit because the wick must burn with joy (in my simple mind) to melt the wax and fuel the fire. We often transferred fire on the farm by wood-flame or candle as matches were pricey. The second aspect of my 'mini-mission' was game-craft to keep the flame alive with a (right, in my case) palm wrap-around to protect the flaming, simultaneously breaking the wind while running at my fastest speed. I practised in the windy farm location. It was tough dealing with the flame, heat and dripping hot wax. My solution – spit on your palms after patting any field soil or mud with both palms and massaging the 'yikes' onto your two hands. The prize was a precious book received by a lightly toasted palm, wax-blisters and a

Quadrant I: Hiking, Fast and in Fear

Quadrant I: Illustrations 10-12

Facing Your Own Demons of Fear

Quadrant I: Illustrations 13-16

Fearless Fight even with Pitching Wedge

hero's welcome from classmates and some well-to-do parents. Thoughtful enthusiasm pays. QED.

Singapore – it's now the 'best place to be born' in this global world – survived whatever afflictions were cast its way and now offers its citizens the bonus of possibly a potential longevity of about a hundred years. Your future, needless to say, is filled with new sensibilities, rich pre-natal and post-natal care, new tech and a time horizon that seems to be shortening between learning and doing, though in more uncertain and complex milieus. But I sense it differently. You're like a quantum sponge taking on more, faster and with the dynamic of a fast accelerator versus the more traditional development-phased incubator. Why? I do not comprehend fully, but this I knew, early. Recall the Grandson & Grandpa Par-3 golfing competition nudged by your foresight-rich Mother (Akela Mum instead of the usual Tiger Mum as described in the later part of this letter) when you were hardly five in about 2012. You managed to shoot out of your first ever bunker which was about twice your height in one shot. U asked how? YY said do exactly as U hit your pitching wedge (not having used a sand wedge) AND finish your swing. U set your stance, popped the ball up and onto the edge of the green and two-putted for a bogey. No fear at all! No hesitation, no doubt, no fear of failure or success! In a simple word – fearless.

Ah-ha, fearlessness is directly from *The Book of Five Rings* — 'The way' ('Tao') of the Samurai of all-time swordsman and writer Miyamoto Musashi: "No fear, no hesitation, no surprise, no doubt." But as you've no ken of that book or the published ideas of Musashi, you just did it without fear of failure or success. U say I mention that many times to you and friends. Yes, I do. I've a lifelong challenge of being in the bunker in courses near and far; and I wish I could do as you did. Sometimes, pals think I have a custom-made sand bunker in my backyard; other times they think I don't practise enough! But when I believe I can do it and finish my swing with my trusty On-Off sand wedge (successor to the Daiwa golf club series), I achieve a high percentage of success. So, I try not to over think or over analyse. Practise, you must. Fearless, you must be. This I unashamedly learnt from U, Jun. But an added case could be made at a higher level, by no other than Christ who said, "I tell you the truth, unless you change and become like little children, you will never enter the kingdom."

Quadrant I: Illustration 17
YY's Adventure Begins

MY EUREKA MOMENT

Some three years later, my fourth shot went into the 18th hole bunker, 5th shot to within five feet of the pin, and one-putt downhill into the hole for bogey 6. And I won the 150th Anniversary Tanglin Club Golf Tourney 2015 Championship at Jurong Golf & Country Club on 38 stableford points on count-back to break the tie! All the practice of that downhill putt using the toe (instead of the mid-point sweet spot) of my beloved 33-inch mallet PRGR putter (lady's model) led to sweet success. Purposeful practice had imparted a benign stroke that created a slower roll but with enough pace to stay faithful along the putting line. There was an ensuing light deceleration unfolding a slight right break-turn into the hole that had been practised hundreds of times – practice that had now paid off! That was in 2015 when as a 71-year old golfer, one could only hope to shoot a nett 71 score with a 25-course handicap. Gross 71 is simply impossible.

That day was magical. However, the heat affected my game in more ways than one. Pars and birdies were hard to come by as the greens were dry and fast and the pin placements were tough. Although it was a real grind, I managed not to lose my beloved start-off pre-experienced Titleist Prov-I ball into any expanse of water, and none ended up OB. In forty years, such luck on the golf course occurred only once. I was mindful of staying in the present amidst emotions running high and drawing from the store of lessons from years of many near wins. However, earlier minor novelty competition wins had helped: longest drive, nearest the line, nearest the par-3 pins (and converting to birdies) in lieu of a hole-in-one (still trying!); and a first 'eagle' on the 310-yard par 4 16th hole at the Macau Golf and Country Club in 1998 with a trusty 4-iron from 150-yards after a mediocre drive playing with my HP-Compaq ichiban Ritter and Fox.

Memories roared back to my 1966 Self-Discovery Outward Bound School Course 112 at Lumut, Perak Darul Ridzuan (Abode of Grace), a state in Malaysia, conjuring up Ulysses' warrior spirit of 'Strive Never Yield'. Climbing Gunung Busu 808 three days in a row was an unending struggle. The Final Test required trekking 30 miles and returning within 9 hours with no team member left behind. Whoa!!! We completed within 15 minutes of the ultimate course-created failure/success deadline! Everyone and everything fell into place, despite the lightning, thunder and rain! Such serendipitous alignment of heaven, earth, man; and a battle won.

If there was an extra factor to that magical day of winning the 150th Anniversary Tanglin Club Golf Tourney in 2015, it is a second memory flashback. I had just bid a sorrowful farewell to my dear late professorial colleague on Bainbridge Island off Seattle, and was returning on Sunday for the mid-week game. He was looking out for me during that game. Fast-forward 45 years from 1969 to 2014, 200 miles south of Des Moines, Iowa to UMKC at Kansas City where I was honouring my same friend. It was just as golfer Ben Crenshaw believed in his mentor, the late peerless golf coach Harvey Penick. Crenshaw had relentlessly inspired the 1999 US Ryder Cup 12 Players who turned around the big deficit on the Sunday and won against a backdrop of having lost two prior consecutive Ryder Cups. Likewise, at the Tanglin Club Charity Open, the Highland Whiskey at the halfway house spurred the spirit of my 14-handicapper golfing partner Yun (who came in third) and myself playing the last five holes swimmingly more relaxed and strangely well. We started parring the Par-3 14th hole across the usually foreboding interloping water – yet it wasn't a factor this time! Yun was on fire with two eagle chances catching two birdies (playing par golf) and this rubbed off on me to playing bogey golf. Together we maintained our paired-momentum generating some sense of confidence which 'magically' melts anxiety (pairing with Tiger Woods is the opposite – it is tension-filled).

I have always thought mutually reinforcing partnership in peace, war, competition, and gamesmanship add to the enjoyment and enhance our chance to be naturally ourselves.

The team is important, but the one thing that will make the difference is U. "There is nothing outside of yourself that can ever enable you to get better, stronger, richer, quicker, or smarter. Everything is within. Everything exists. Seek nothing outside of yourself," according to Miyamoto Musashi.

From your early readings of Greek philosophy, mythology and traditions even the Oracle of Delphi opines, "Know thyself" while Sun Tzu reflects, "Know yourself. A hundred battles, a hundred victories."

Always remember there are multiple ways up any mountain. The easy, the tried, the unexpected and the improbable – just as Mr Alex Honnold faced when he fearlessly free-solo climbed the sheer cliff face of El Capitan in Yosemite National Park without harness or ropes!

AGE FOR AGE AND THE FUTURE UNKNOWN?

I was so struck that our paths crossed at an early age, Jun, you at about 4 and YY at 68. As you read through this letter, you might notice that I think of you and your cousins highly. Age for age till 12, I concede with grace that you and Cousin Xuan beat me in smarts and achievement; and ever so tech-savvy! And yet, inter-generationally we can still learn from each other – as hopefully this letter would show with some clarity and some directional sense rather than precision.

Looking back, a 2018 issue of the *New England Journal of Medicine* indicated that retirement may not be a good choice as the most productive years of a human's life are from age 60 to 70. Episodically, the average age of a Nobel Winner and *Fortune 500* CEO is respectively about 62 to 63. In a later part of this letter, I describe serendipitously my most enjoyable and successful projects that led to winning the national Chingay Champion Float in 2009 and the IOC commendation for the NTU-YOG Village in 2010. YY was then in his 60s. I won't go into detail here, because you could just read on (and like the mystery movie as to who did it? 'No, no don't tell me!').

That's why I am emphatic that you need to exude from yourself sustainable enthusiasm to carry you through from age 12 to 70 and beyond, as your generation could have longevity of 100 years! Enthusiasm said, when asked how I was accepted by two premier post-graduate universities of highest repute, I replied to Lee Foundation Chairman Dr Lee Seng Tee that I was lucky because I knew there are folks who're much smarter than me. He cryptically said, "Better lucky than smart. Still got to work hard" (my comment, "That's normal").

In my bones, I have hope and faith that you're *'fearlessly' different* and when you set your mind to what you wish for, you will roll with the punches of life as in golf.

An Aside: Fortune sat me next to the hallowed Honourable Peter Lougheed MBA'51 (former Premier of Alberta and the PM that Canada never had) who asked me at the time of the NAFTA negotiations conducted by artful negotiator Simon Reisman, what advice I had for him. O, me with meagre talent said: "No more Mr Nice Guy, Sir." Never ever would I have dreamt of Trudeau versus Trump two decades later. To his "How so?" retort, I summoned enough voice to say, "If it pleases you, I'll send you *The Book of Five Rings*." And I spent a week hunting for a copy to send him. It was his minute of intense engagement where you're intuitively rated. I guess I passed as he gave me an appointment and with his quiet charm, subsequently received me in his law offices.

If the mandate is from Heaven, Heaven be praised for Trudeau Senior and successor Trudeau Junior in the great tradition of a more just and more equal society with strong moral leadership amongst our leading global leaders. With the onset of 'Trumpism' since 2016 like the era of President Andrew Jackson in the 1800s, hopefully there will be a swing back to the values of America's other early pioneers like Alexander Hamilton, Thomas Jefferson and 20th century 'new deal' F.D. Roosevelt. Our

Quadrant I: Illustrations 18-19
Onward & Upward many Paths

human civilisation depends on maintaining the values of a just and equal society and strong leadership for our own survival in the face of climate change deniers as our little blue planet continues to heat up; and surprises, unknown.

GENESIS OF THIS LETTER

I Found Myself Hiking at 1, 3 to 100mph.

I thought I had found myself whilst hiking and fast driving. But philosophers, psychologists and opinion-givers admonish: Think again! So, I revisit my early hiking memories.

Hiking 10 and 20 miles at 1mph: reality versus classroom learning debunks the truism that the shortest route is as the crow flies. For the starter hiker, the reality is that every 'straight crow-fly mile' is about 1.6 miles after obstacles and detours.

Accidental Hike: When I was about nine years old, I found my own way home by walking five miles. I had waited for my eldest brother to go home together. He was delayed some hour and a half which had never happened before. It must have been something important. So I thought I might just walk the five miles home by retracing the more direct bus route to school in reverse – which wasn't as the crow flies! It took me about two hours after spending a third of the time stopping to view the river boats (colourful wooden 'tongkangs'), activities by the bridge, the

Quadrant I: Illustrations 20-22
Hiking & Climbing

crowded wet market, retail shops, biscuit and oil tin container-makers, old coffeeshops of all descriptions, rice-traders with gunny sacks all stacked up, a Chinese temple with fearsome deities, devotees in prayer with burning joss sticks and a monk in a trance, also a mosque, a church and a Hindu temple. Following the sequence of bus stops, I eventually reached home! My brother turned up soon after and was relieved to see me at dinner with our family. I whispered to him, that walking home alone was not a big deal – in fact thanks to him I had experienced the local geography of cultural and economic activity. It did give me a sudden boost of self-confidence. It was a happy day for all – was this the beginnings of my hiking streak?

Early Hiking Years: From the age of 9, I would hike in groups on day trips. At 11, I ventured on overnight hikes in smaller groups. By the time I was a teenager, it was more exciting being a journeyman co-hiker as a Junior Scout for my 10-mile First Class Badge and eventually as a Senior Scout for my 20-mile Venture Class Badge to gain the ultimate Queen's Scout Badge.

I remember my very first First-Class hike as a journeyman partner and guide to my classmate and pal Kiat Siong (eventually christened by our Commissioner as 'Kemo-Sabe' or 'Trusty Scout' in Texas Red Indian language) tracking through belukar-clad gullies. We hiked from Pasir Panjang through Jurong to Tengah along the swampy river by Lorong Tengah to a 'camp-site' by the village retail shop whose owner invited us to stay in his loft which we graciously declined, 'scout's honour'.

Quadrant I: Illustrations 23-28
Visualising my Favourite Raven

The next day we tracked to Choa Chu Kang Road and on to Hong Kah, then hiking to Upper Bukit Timah near Bukit Gombak. Ever on the lookout for the quarry (we checked and avoided the blasting times though that's the sound of music in a distance), the high telecoms tower, and the majestic Albizia trees by Gombak along Upper Bukit Timah Road.

FORWARD LOOKING & FAR HORIZONS

You plan your hiking route in daylight from about 8a.m. to 4p.m. with leeway of an hour to divvy into five discrete mini-mission stages a mile at a time. These stages are intended as the route, using markers or milestones to align the trek as opposed to the map route, to avoid going too far off the rails. It's a basic five miles hiked over secondary forest, bush and secondary roads at a steady pace (with a factor of 1.6 for deviations by design or accident making it 8 miles) or a running rate of a mile per hour to make camp by 5p.m., set up tent-camp, cook dinner, debrief and plan for the next day. Our hiking journeyman calls up precocious 'adult supervision', overseeing terrain and time management; safety, health and hydration; the backwoods man cooks the nutrition (rucksack limited) and is the 'guardian angel'.

Accumulated hike hours make you bolder and wiser than your age (at times you feel that you possess more 'power' as in your computer games). You worry beyond what your eyes can see and use your growing perception

Quadrant I: Illustration 29
Feel Earth & Seek Landmarks

through your mind's eye. You rise to a higher helicopter view of the mission and your legs seem to grow stronger, feeling and reading the shifty ground. Sometimes, however, experience unquestioned is a dangerous thing just as memories of the past are. This is because the problem before us may be totally new and needing a fresh look forward rather than harking backward to solutions that may be outdated and muddied by changing underlying circumstances.

So the 20-mile Venture Hike is not only about building up stamina and a pace to exceed 1mph; more importantly, it is the will to cope with lengthening far horizons. It's akin in retrospect to the marathon runner. He doesn't practise running the whole 42km again and again. Runs are calibrated for pace, race strategy, terrain factor, and stamina build-up with the will to replicate and run the eventual marathon.

The Accumulated Experience is one hundred percent of no health issues and of successful completions. Till today my friend Uncle Chuan Lock from my Primary 1 class and scout troop is a happy camper and hiker with me. "Memories are made of this" sang Dean Martin more than 68 years ago. Uncle Chuan and I also have fond memories of the complaet and expressive Mrs Chelvan who was our first grade class teacher. We knew when she was angry ("Holy anger," she would say) rather often but always with a dose of love and 'Mother-care'.

I THOUGHT I FOUND MYSELF HIKING

I thought I found myself hiking until I met fear and broke the fear barrier. It was fear of the unknown in my twenties: you meet first the idea of who you think you are! It's discomfiting to realise that you do face fear. I feared jumping into the middle of the Pangkor Straits along the well-known Straits of Malacca (between Pangkor Island and the Malayan Peninsula by Perak reportedly deep with sharks and all) but it was only a chest deep sand bank! It was embarrassing but true fear showed all of us up (none jumped into the water on command) during the one-month self-discovery programme at the Outward Bound School in Lumut, Perak. We were fearful even under the guidance and obvious assessment of experienced instructors. In charge was the no-nonsense pipe-smoking Sherlock Holmes-nesque Warden John W. Tucker. He was a tough officer, sailor and mountaineer, tasked to break our existent spirit and innermost hidden being to enable our 'new self' to emerge. He was to provide the highly sought final written insight as to whether we were made of sterner stuff to the companies and uniformed services who sponsored our section members. It was like telling us to overcome yesterday's self, renew today and be ready the next day for the world! That's a tall order, so I was of course worried. Nevertheless, I put my full heart into this one-month trial by 'new' pathless waters, lands, flora, fauna, and forested skies to cooperating with new colleagues and self! Fortune smiled and I was awarded a Merit Badge - Course 112.

I was naturally pleased with the citation of being a good trekker: "A good scout who has good knowledge of map reading and compass bearing. He was very keen during the expedition (the 30-mile trek) and he drives hard." What surprised me was the Warden's comment of a good and trusted companion in sailing. I did not sink the ketch with the full-course cohort when helming it along the mid-stream with the constancy of a hiker's immovable far-off horizon's mountain marker as a steady line regressing to the mean. I successfully navigated the ketch into the mouth of the turbulent Perak River from the placid Straits of Malacca under the watchful eye of the warden-sailor. Best of all, his report cited a level of 'savoir faire': "Some mistook him (*me*) as a member of the OBS staff team!" Appreciatively, I told my instructors who kept in touch during visits in the ensuing years that such flatteries were pleasingly noted and accepted with grace especially the words shown lots of enthusiasm.

The Arabs talk about the idea awe or *'hayba'* – the aura of leadership. Chancellor Cao Cao of *The Three Kingdoms* epic historist-novella speaks of the 'reddened aura' exuded in the face of warrior Guan Yu. Some may think this is a new phenomenon but it's not. Nowadays there are the Bandai Gundam toys and game figurine series. You've got to be able to identify visually, but more importantly in your mind's eye, who these individuals are, be they your colleagues, competitors, rivals, et al. Hopefully by such an understanding, you develop your defences and coping skills whilst you accelerate acquiring such a quality of perception.

Question Zero: What do you seek to find, challenge and perhaps change? Is it to expand and strengthen the breadth, depth and sinew of the internal spirit?

Quadrant I: Illustration 30
Can do. Boleh!

BREAKING THE FEAR BARRIER AGAIN

I thought that I had broken the fear barrier at an early age of about six when I accompanied my eldest brother Keng walking home from school. On our way home passing several farms near the main Changi Road, our neighbour's dog in the presence of his owners barked unusually aggressively. Suddenly the dog attacked my Brother and bit him on the left ankle. Keng, falling backwards and lengthening his left leg to ease the drag of the bite, arched his body backwards, grabbed a nearby stick and mightily whacked the dog between the shoulder and back hump giving off a bone-crackling sound. There were whining yelps of the humbled dog scampering away wounded and with its tail between its legs while our neighbours were aghast and proffering platitudes. I felt that I was lifted from fear, of dogs or any bully. In the adrenaline of faith, the experience aroused no fear of any tasks laid or thrown in my way. Years later, I remembered this incident well. I had been tasked with delivering a message from the 4th Bangkok National Jamboree 1961 (where I was the distinctly uniformed Singapore Contingent Patrol Leader) to the gate-less Lien (Ying Chow) Holland Villa in Singapore. Unexpectedly I came face to face with two black Rottweilers charging down the unusual pinkish brick driveway. I stayed calm maintaining eye-contact and unmoving till the maid servant hollered at them to heel and welcomed me to hand over the message.

As narrated earlier, I had also experienced a breaking of the fear barrier while hiking over the unknown countryside of Singapore in the early 1950s and 1960s in the middle of the Pangkor Straits at the Outward

Quadrant I: Illustrations 31-32
Squid Fear: Jump or Trampoline

Bound School. The lesson for me is the need to revisit and be self-reflective so that complacency doesn't set in. More importantly we must nurture to grow our inner strength against fear and the usually unexpected crisis which presents both danger, fear of danger and challenge of opportunity.

Low Bars & Low Distances

It's not the distance of the goal that matters, because when you reach it you may have set too low a bar. But I intuitively kept going, ranging from 10 miles in my scouting days, to 30-mile group hike-treks. Soon I could complete a hike in the Perak jungles by returning within 9 hours ahead of any of the 12-team members. Eventually as a young executive I achieved a first time ever 3,000 miles fast 'hike-driving' across America!

30-Mile Trek & Full Team Returning in 9 Hours: For this hugely never attempted daunting 30-mile task, I was now fitter after an intense three weeks of a daily physical regimen and terrain familiarity making a more direct 3-mph pace possible with mounting pressure and tension. In my mind's eye runs the Ulysses of *The Illiad* retold in poetry by Lord Tennyson:

> *'One equal temper of heroic hearts*
>
> *Made weak by time and fate* **but strong in will**
>
> *To strive, to seek, to find and not to yield.'*

Beyond the Compass, the GPS: A new reality emerged on the 30-mile task. It was well assayed by the seasoned OBS trainers who would reward accuracy of terrain reading and hitting the 'not so obvious' key markers along the way. Such an approach was to enable a truer '30-mile race trekking course' without being saddled with the 1.6 obstacle-avoidance factor as in my earlier 10 to 20-mile hikes.

Kasich's Question Zero: 'Who is the compass-man?' so said Ohio Governor John Kasich at Harvard Kennedy School of Government's Convocation 2018. I am the compass-man and even at the age of 22 in 1966, my preferred persona is to be the innate GPS-man (GPS wasn't invented then) which I am not but ever willing to learn. I found myself to be a competent compass-man in tracking over 10,000 hours including the jungles of inland Perak by Lumut. But my Dayak Pal Mike Sairin whose

Quadrant I: Illustrations 33-34
Fast Forward Boston: Creative Fear, Learning & Driving

life and generations past, trekked and survived daily in the jungles of Borneo had nature's gift of a GPS-feel for the terrain in light or darkness. Whilst in late afternoon darkening foliage cover, he saved us by shouting in colloquial Malay from the rear that we should be on the ascent not descent. Gosh, he was right, though my compass pointed me correctly, but my rechecking of the 'topo' map showed that we had overshot by about 150 yards (they didn't care for metres those days) in forest cover over a knoll and going downhill – tired legs and disorientation in early tones of dusk. A needed retracing and our lucky turning point was cutting through the secondary forest cover, and seeing a 'zinc roof' reflecting the sunlight. Thinking it to be a house, we discovered it was actually a sunlit pond, as in the topo map with an adjacent secondary road to our camp destination. We then raced back at full speed to complete the 30-mile mission within fifteen minutes of the 9-hour deadline.

How Did We Manage 3-mph Pace: Dayak Mike and I earned the team members' respect. Mike could feel GPS and visualise? I could compass-topo and visualise. We were fortunate to have been able to visualise in our mind's eye. We didn't know it then, but some people cannot visualise mental images. They might do it another way like Pixar's co-founder Ed Catmull an award winning animator. Fast forward, read "Aphantasia" in <https://www.bbc.com/news/health-47830256> where Catmull says 'my mind's eye is blind'.

In a month we had earned our spurs. However, it was not before we needed to straighten out our unmotivated 12th member, Master Nephew accompanied by his motivated 'chaperon' Mr Uncle. We did the first mile in thirty minutes or 2mph (at that pace we would only make 18 to 20 miles, not 30 in 9 hours and fail the test) as we had to carry and cajole Nephew. It was a more than daunting task now, but we all agreed (Uncle included) that Dayak Mike with his nature's 'wild & fierce' mien would pep talk Nephew with a proposition: we were all willing to fail (he didn't seem too impressed, and rightly so as we wanted success badly). But we couldn't carry on like this. We'd leave him by the watering hole in the jungle opening with enough food and water, trek without him and pick him up on our way back. Hopefully, the animals coming to drink wouldn't mistake him as an added special offering for their meal of the day! There were footprints of mousedeer, wild-boars and sun-bears, (tigers and lions too, Nephew wouldn't know the difference.)

Mike gave him five minutes to think it over and we proceeded to pick up pace. And lo! He voted with his feet ! So we assigned him our strongest team member, a Federal Military College military cadet, to be his guardsman to ensure the running-rate pace to D-Day Hour 9. And we all passed including our 'saviour' No.12!

What's the secret ? It is Creative Fear – also practised at the well-known Eastern (Atlantic seaboard) Harvard Business School HBS as I was to find out the following year!

Quadrant II
Driving, Faster and Farther

Dream Far

The pathos of distance reveals the suffering and experience of hikes and drives starting from 10 miles, to 20, then 30 and eventually to a 3,000-mile hike-drive! How did this quantum leap come about? From 1mph for a 10 to 20-mile hike to 3mph for a 30-mile endurance trek-hike-run to a hundred-fold 3,000-mile hike-drive hitting 100mph?

This rhythm of faster and farther is a huge stretch into a kaleidoscope of colours of a continent!

Jun, for me it was a chemistry of a surreal, twilight zone out-of-body suspense. To say that it was unearthly is not right, as Soong had done it before and so had the Cimarron pioneers. But it had a mix of oriental duality – east-west and 'Go West & the Sutra' (the oriental legends of the *Journey to the West* by the Monkey God) to latter-day western cowboys.

The east-west tilt beneath the big skies is seen in the contrasting duo-cities of worldly New York on the Atlantic and Asia-facing effervescent San Francisco on the Pacific (as in old China, beneath heaven are duet jewels of Hangzhou and Suzhou like so: 上有天堂, 下有苏杭).

Driving from the East Coast to the West Coast was a giant leap from the trusty pre-used chariot of fire, a Ford Comet of my roommate Toby Canto. Compare his car to the new-tech auto-horses of Soong's BMW 2002ti and his pal's iconic Lee Iaccoca classic Ford Mustang Cobra. Cruising along our nearby easterly New England roads admiring the riot of colours of autumn along the way, our meeting-up point was at East Lansing, Michigan on the western road across 'continental' America.

I had actually been preparing to go back to SG to marry my hometown sweetheart (YY's Margaret Cheang, now Grandma). But running into classmate Leo Soong hailing from the parkland of Stanford and legendary city of St Francis, San Francisco, beckoned me, "Hey Tony, 'tis a chance of a lifetime! Need to co-drive sometimes!"

For YY, it was Wow! It felt like striking the lottery (in Fukien ~ teo beh poey!).

Somehow, sometimes our past links into the present. Being a graduate member in residence at the Business School in Soldiers Field Boston has its benefits. Kresge (aka 'chow-house') is the central collegiate dining hall enabling agoraphobic exchanges of ideas and experiences. Leo Soong spoke about the riotous colours of New England's Fall '68. I related riding in a Trans-Am to Montreal with 'mon ami' Québécois Jeff Mudge. There had also been an earlier summer drive in a Pontiac-Catalina from New York City to Niagara and back as a solo US-licensed driver with my dear summer-intern Mobil Oil colleague Singaporean Tony Choy. There was a spring drive with section-mate Rich Wilson in his fireman-red Camaro to his East Tennessee home in Johnson City and for me, an experience of the amazing quilt of colours and wonders of the interstate highways.

Leo cryptically said, "You ain't seen nothing yet." Not till his call to co-drive from New York City to San Francisco, did it all finally click!

And I said yes without hesitation nor a second thought but with a rush of enthusiasm. Soong knew I was serious – a done deal with a handshake! We

Quadrant II: Illustration 1
Beaming I-80 Indy 3,000: NYC-San Francisco

intuitively felt a kindred spirit that brought about a feeling of mutual comfort riding across the continental Great Plains from sea to shining sea; from Old Boston whaling station to new San Francisco where, by the Pacific lake, the tourists view the annual migrating whales in nuclear family pods.

Had I practised with purpose? Luckily, I may have – prepping for the major marathon with mini marathons. For drives, I did sign on with folks with whom I felt a kindred spirit. They included fellow Kresge diners like doctoral Jeff and section-mate Tennessee-an Rich for whom I became his working visa to travel. To secure his beloved aging Mother's assent, Rich would tell her, "I'm going to see Tony" (the only Chinese person she had ever met in her life at Johnson City, Tennessee). He once flew from Houston to Hong Kong on a super-offer via Continental Airlines. We had cool times to reciprocate his southern hospitality with the eastern charm of Fragrant Harbour aka Hong Kong whilst Macau reminded him of Atlantic City. At the Outward Bound School in my earlier days of hiking, it was just luck of the draw that determined which diverse group of youths you had to join, none of whom I had met before. In such groups you had only a short time to build the comradeship, usually over a rhythm of four weeks into a month's programme.

O Lady Luck (Machiavelli describes Fortune as a woman): My thoughts vividly hark back to my boyhood imagination of the mid-1955 Todd AO 70mm magnificent wide-screen Rodgers and Hammerstein's musical *Oklahoma*, a film that I saw in a local cinema. I can still recall the feeling of joy as the movie took us riding across endless golden cornfields in a surrey with a fringe on the top with happy cowboys and cowgirls. Likewise were my recollections of the new-1960s icon of Peter Fonda's movie, *Easy Rider*, as two bikers rode across country and desert lands.

In my mind's eye, my vision of a co-drive from New York City to San Francisco needed some quick readjustments. It was not entirely as seen in the movies. There would be the shared cost of driving and flying back to Boston for Commencement to receive my scroll as evidence of completion. And to finance this unexpected opportunity, I had to borrow S$1,500 from the United Bank of Roxbury – unsecured and thankfully evidenced only by my good American Express Gold Card, issued by Watertown Bank Harvard Square Branch. Unreservedly, I determined to go on this journey in the scouting spirit, over 3,000 miles of rolling hills and dales (and in the spirit of Aeneas from Troy to Italia, Jun, as in your reading of Homer's *Iliad* and Virgil's *Aeneid*). Our drive was to take us to San Francisco where Amadeo Pietro Giannini founded the little Bank of Italy and shot to fame by financing whosoever committed to rebuild in a speedy couple of days after the Great Quake of 1906. That Bank of Italy later merged with the Bank of America Los Angeles to become the one and only Bank of America, NT&SA (National Trust and Savings Association). It was emulated by the trusted OCBC Bank after the ravages of WWII in 1945 Singapore. In the early 1950s, the Lee Family through their Lee Rubber Company founded the social enterprise, the Lee Foundation that generously supported civic and community welfare. The Lee Foundation generously provided the historic and huge $150 million endowment to the NTU-Imperial College Lee Kong Chian School of Medicine (through the aegis of Dr Lee Seng Tee and SR Nathan, then Chancellor of the Nanyang Technological University) in about 2010. (YY had a little something to do with this as part of the ruling NTU

Quadrant II: Illustration 2

Onwards towards the Jackalope Trail!

Discovery Drive~1,000 Leagues across America

Troika.) This School of Medicine successfully graduated the 2018 pioneer first cohort of 52 nuevo health system doctors dually able to practise in the UK and SG thrusting our regional medical hub into a leading edge. Similarly, as gratitude to his alma mater NTU and Cambridge, the valedictorian Dr Leon Tan was the first-stage winner of the endowed ASC Teo & Dr Gordon Johnson Gold Medal. The second stage is the inaugural LKCSM-Wolfson Clinical Internship at Cambridge and the new Bio-Med Campus which encompasses Addenbrookes Hospital will be awarded in 2022 (postponed from 2020 owing to COVID-19).

In truth, the 3,000-mile hike-drive yielded manifold returns as you will find in this letter. I never repeated the trip but the experience continues to sink in after all these 50 years. I keep drawing new takeaways from it when I address my undergraduates and graduates, most recently at the Lee Kuan Yew School of Public Policy (LKY-SPP) in April 2019. Then on my sojourn farthermost south to NZ's southern city of Queenstown (a stone's throw away from Antarctica) where serendipitously, and beyond any belief, I met the early new future when the first river, River Whanganui, became a Legal Person. Fast forward just a peek, I did find myself hiking, again trekking up one of its many peaks but ever always seeking, discovering and creating, hopefully engaging the future before too long.

My 3,000-mile hike-drive no doubt spurred me on to setting up, upon my return to Singapore, an Alumni 'Open-Horizon' S$1,500 Travel Grant Programme at Harvard itself. Two most famous 1970s recipients were Harvard College Chen Shao Mao, a lawyer turned politician and Chan Suling from the Law School to full-time mother and managing her family philanthropy Mead-Chan Foundation based out of London, UK. My thanks to our network of friends as with the late Eliot House Master Alan Heimert and Arline for their adroit administering of the award with a high sense of joy in helping graduates find their own self-discovery journey of pursuing their favoured 'Moby Dick' voyages (Heimert is the all-time American scholar of American Literature whose genre straddles that of the renaissance author Herman Melville and on).

Then the onset of reality sank in. In my mind, I had flashes of 100 mini-missions of riding across our homeland, the 30-mile wide island of Singapore, as the visceral intuition for the 'pathos of distance' of 3,000 miles kicked in (an idea that rationalised itself 50 years after). The wild, wild west was to be revisited on auto-steeds with the speed of

Quadrant II: Illustrations 3-4
Rapid 600-mile: NYC to Holy Toledo!

Quadrant II: Driving, Faster and Farther

Quadrant II: Illustration 5
Mighty Mississippi!

the arrow (as in the word Cimarron) or fast summer lightning, in poetic Shakespeare!

Soong was great, he let me drive his favourite steed. He rode it best and my word, expertly! In fleeting moments, in the inward eye there are flashes of the early pioneering wagons off the beaten tracks often in the wilderness led by the outriders on horses with tired backs, bowed legs and sore buns. We have it easy!

We were on the road less travelled, driving from NYC to SF on Interstate 1-80 (some mistakenly cite the American humourist Will Rogers romanticised Route 66 from the Mid-West on a south-westerly route to Los Angeles). At the wheel was seasoned auto-ist Soong replete with racer-gloves in his favourite BMW 2002ti covering 3,000 miles or about 3,600 miles after detours crossing twelve states. Our journey took us from New York, then on to Pennsylvania, Ohio, a detour to East Lansing in Michigan to rendezvous with our added self-insurance of having pre-med driver II Frank, back to

Indiana, Illinois, Iowa, Nebraska, Wyoming, Utah, Nevada and eventually to California through its capital Sacramento to San Francisco.

Route 66 is recounted in John Steinbeck's classic, *The Grapes of Wrath*, that focused on escape and loss. Our Soong-YY I-80 was about Soong's highway to home and YY's sense of adventure in finding himself hiking. In this case YY was going faster and farther, driving perchance a bonus to gel and imagine the reality towards discovering the "idea of America" rather than just a travelogue. This astounding spiderweb-like network of US highways was unique till the PRC exceeded it in length and connectivity in about the year 2000.

Big Skies, Big Country: Big cities transitioned to vastness of the land, skies, prairies, bountiful wheat, corn & soybeans, unending ranges of mountains, salt lakes & deserts, and the Sierra Nevada of the 'huge country-like' California. We pass huge Cimarron trailers like auto-steed and trains or 'iron-horses' on rails built a hundred years ago. We are on endless highways that we share with the huge road-runners dispensing 'whiplash' upon smaller vehicles as they speed by. Truckers race in their gigantic new Paccar premium vehicles, custom-made by Seattle-based Kenworth & Peterbilt (Jun, they are like your transformer truck toys). The supply chain of these trucks serves huge and far flung markets that every trading country wants a piece of. These are the new 'auto-horses' that run on the interwoven networks of highways. Alaska has high-pay high-risk drivers who 'drive at your own risk' on remote ice-lake roads to reach the Arctic supply centres. Incidentally, this is not new – it's like your computer game of Genghis Khan's battles in the west along Euro-Asia, fighting in the deep of winter when the Mongol armies and supply horses ran on hard frozen and even 'river-roads' avoiding the muddy roads ahead.

In visual form, the tracks of the limited rail-based trains are like special sutures on the human body versus the network of veins of highways. To own a vehicle and drive is as Americana as the right to bear arms according to the Second Amendment of the U.S. Constitution. A li'l lesson from this east-west hike-drive is that Americans have low personal tolerance for poor drivers not poor driving! It's Americana's Rorschach test for manhood for all; and for truckers, livelihood and brotherhood on the highway.

At remote service stops (or 'third' spaces of respite) we shared the truckers' fare of greasy bacon and eggs with strong coffee that looked like dish water. Tough guys. Tough life. We have it easy as easy riders in a BMW (in Seattle, it means the economy driven by Boeing, Microsoft & Weyerhaeuser). But we kept a fast pace with grace and respect negotiating the straight stretches and curvy bends. Imperceptibility, we gradually gained acceptance in their brotherhood on the long interstate highways. The truckers' own sense of their classic top-of-the-line Seattle-produced Kenworth truck (which is their preferred colourful Appaloosa horse) is akin to our pal Frank's timeless black Mustang Cobra. He joined us on the road after East Lansing in Michigan where we started our two-some car teams of Soong-Teo and Frank cruising 2,000 miles to San Francisco.

These thoughts and memories come flooding back in wide 'Vista-Vision' or 'Cinema-Scope'. I see the living colours and natural sound-surround of America across the 3,000-mile east-west spectrum along four thematic story boards:

1. *Rust, Agri-USA & Future Valleys*: Memories of riding through the rust belt of Pennsylvania reflected the troubled steel industry profiled by the Harvard Business School (HBS) case-study of the U.S. steel industry of the 1960s (even then). I recall readings on the leading trade union leader Walter Reuther's campaign to earlier times of the 1960's versions of 'making America great again'.

With a rush of adrenaline, we exceeded the advice of yore that a journey of a thousand miles starts with a single step. We surprised ourselves that a journey of 3,000 miles starts off with a sustained 600 miles in the first 12 hours at speeds varying from 60-100 mph! (Trekking nine continuous hours in the Perak jungles resurfaced as an anchor-experience!) We travelled accident-free from NYC to Toledo, Ohio home of once *Fortune 500* Champion Spark Plug founded in 1908. An update would tell of the company's fortune and ownership that changed owing to technological change. But the Toledo Mud Hens Baseball Team founded in 1883 survives and thrives in the Triple A League supplying talent to Major League Baseball superhero Detroit Tigers World Champions'68. Pointedly, the winning Tigers Champion Team included the local favourite son Tommy Matchick with his legendary all-round skills, derring-do and raring to go enthusiasm – ever-ready to substitute and seamlessly execute team-play plans at a moment's notice. The Mud Hens were the

Quadrant II: Illustrations 6-7
Twin Easy Riders: BMW 2002 & Mustang Cobra at East Lansing, MI

undisputed Americana's field of dreams and hero City-zen of Toledo (as Red Sox is the dynastic superhero to Boston), more later. Wow! Am I doing this?

The takeaway is that baseball and driving are continental America's core litmus tests towards an all-America identity. Essentially, especially for driving – if you can't drive, you ain't going nowhere and in earlier days, if you don't ride no horse, you ain't nothing, too!

The golden fields of Iowa are akin to a fieldtrip on burgeoning corporate agri-business as preached by the lonely voice in the new wilderness in the person of HBS pioneer Agri-Business Professor Ray Goldberg. There is the visual growing tension with the traditional smaller-scale rural family farms and the discomforting trade-off between corn as a family staple-food versus as an ethanol energy mix for the auto and maturing oil industries, increasingly chased down by cleaner fuels. To this day Iowa is now the soy and corn granary of America made more famous by the visit to Muscatine in 1983 of a young agri-business commissar (who later became PRC's President Xi). Muscatine is located en route from Chicago three hours to Des Moines. The then Governor was Terry Branstad (later U.S. Ambassador to Beijing from 2017 to 2020). Fast forward, when Xi was asked why on his visit in 2012 before becoming PRC President he went to Muscatine instead of Washington, D.C., he said, "But, this is America (heartland)."

This is, indeed, the heartland of pioneers! Then unbeknownst to me fast-forward again 45 years later to 2014, I flew a farther 15,000 kilometres (5,000km short of semi-circumnavigation) on a 20-hour risky short-transit connected flights from Singapore, Tokyo, Chicago to Kansas City (which is 200 miles south of Des Moines). I was to deliver the keynote address for my NTU colleague who was then Dr TK Tan, Dean of the Bloch Business School, University of Missouri-Kansas City (UMKC). Dr Tan was being honoured by his patron Dr Henry Bloch, philanthropist and founder of expert tax preparer H&R Block by naming the cathedral atrium of his $32-million UMKC's Entrepreneurs' & Innovators' Experiential Center after him. Like the 3,000-mile drive with Soong, this trip was undertaken spontaneously, on TK's phone call invitation. In a voice of enthusiasm, I responded, "Yes, I will come." TK knew that I would certainly come.

Quadrant II: Illustrations 8-9
Cheyenne: Mile High Top of the World at El Rancho

Quadrant II: Illustration 10
Magnificent North Star & Soong's Unbeknownst
Star Renaissance Man

Jun, in life there are times when you need to do what you need to do. When your best pal is quintessentially honoured in the land of highly regarded business schools (and in cruel happenstance, he was just diagnosed with 4th stage pancreatic cancer), you need to honour the call. This pal-ship is personally so special that I refer to it several times as I fast forward re-connecting the strings (with hindsight). In late 2015, in a golf competition TK had my back, calmed the butterflies-in-my-stomach and eased me in by a whisker to my first ever tournament win after 40 years of tuition fees paid to countless golf courses.

All who attended the gathering in Kansas City were surprised that I would honour my pal's clarion call. Whilst I was in awe of the love that all had for TK, setting aside my notes I delivered an impromptu and emotive three-minute oration to deafening applause (accentuated by my errant ear after so many hours on an aeroplane). Present also were dignitaries including the UMKC Chancellor, President, Patron, and alumni as well as

Quadrant II: Illustrations 11-12
Riding Reno to the Golden Gate Bridge to Asia

Esther George President & CEO of the Federal Reserve Bank of Kansas City. Asked by the presiding Chancellor to choose a word that aptly captures the spirit of TK, I selected 'dangerous' (to laughter and claps). In the epistemology of the concept of 'crisis' it is depicted as danger with opportunity in Chinese calligraphy. When a faraway faculty eyed him as 'dangerous' for his proclivity to embrace rapid change, UMKC with 25,000-graduate studentship saw him as an opportunity to redefine the business school into a leading entrepreneurship & innovation centre. Such a bold move was in sync with the KC spirit as a pioneering hub ever since its frontier days as the nexus of railroad, agriculture and animal vet-hygiene distribution – a key node of 'Heartland USA'. TK assiduously reinforced this centrality to which the City and UMKC responded with celebrated acclaim. He soothed all egos and integrated all these into a vibrant eco-system as KC is also the home of the globally reputed Kauffman Foundation dedicated to the promotion of entrepreneurship. We also maintain a continuing conversation through the Marion and Henry Bloch Family Foundation that supports post-secondary and entrepreneurship education.

2. *Old & Future Valleys:* As we climbed up the Sierra Nevada (after the dry Utah salt lakes and Nevada desert via Reno), we had our first peek ahead of California. Towards Sacramento in the valley below, atop Yosemite National Park you see the gigantic sequoias that tower 300 feet. Visually, birds disappear to the plains giving way to the forest where the ever-present summertime 'Smoky the Bear', the patron-preventer of forests aflame in the drier climes, reminds hikers and picnickers against fire hazard habits. What an experience to have viewed the contrasting vista of the East coast where the forests in New England are aflame in a riot of autumn colours whilst in the Carolinas, the Smoky Mountains are honeymoon resorts (so went my dear pal Tony Choy and his lovely bride from New York City) with the intervening Appalachian Trails to boot.

Water inequality is apparent in the westerly part of the 3,500-mile wide I-80 that took us winding about mountains and highlands! That area misses the main flow of the mighty Mississippi and its generous waters and periodic floods. If trees could talk as in Tolkien's epic of Middle-earth, they could tell the tale. The giant sequoia trees would share their history as do their accumulated tree-rings around their girth. The rings record the periods of drier climates and droughts that sometimes stretched over

20, 30 to a hundred years as in the middle ages. Some sequoias have even lived for more than a thousand years!

Whereas Boston and New York have an abundant snowy winter wonderland, from the Sierra you can see the snow-capped high Mount Shasta and the nearby Yosemite peaks that hide a much-needed key water source of snow-packs for California's fertile San Joaquin Valley. The scenery transitions to the promise of California in the parklands of 'Harvard of the West' Stanford and Palo Alto (versus the dense city of Cambridge MA centred at Harvard Square). Palo Alto saw the four-decade rise of Silicon Valley in about 1978, and where Apple eventually became the first trillion dollar corporate giant in about 2018 – rather like the Biblical 40-year sojourn of Moses in the Sinai to the Promised Land. So walked another legend, Marc Andreessen who hitched-hike from Iowa's Cedar Falls to Palo Alto and founded Netscape – the Internet mouse, now more famous than Mickey Mouse. And from FedEx, there was CEO Jim Barksdale who in an interview with *AsianBusiness* highlighted his leading role as 'adult supervision' of the bevy of young talent and creators amongst whom was Brendan Eich who created the 'JavaScript'. Perpendicular along the coastline runs Interstate I-5 connecting Silicon Valley up north to Portland (location of Nike Factory Store) to Seattle (location of Microsoft that became a trillion-dollar giant in 2019 after dominating cloud computing), all the way to Vancouver in British Columbia, Canada. In the east, the earlier semi-circle valley was Route 128 around Boston, dominated by Harvard and MIT.

3. *De Tocqueville's Village Church & Fount of Democracy:* In Salt Lake City, the heartland of the Mormons, there is the awe inspiring Salt Lake Temple with its golden angel Moroni on the top spire. Along north Nevada across Elko County is Rexburgh Idaho where HBS Dean Kim Clarke took up as head of Brigham Young U in about 2006 – having left his deanship at HBS with complete obedience, a trait not intuitively American!

We drove by Elko and struck the jackpot on the first pull of quarters or 25-cent slot machine. (Our winnings later came to good use at the town of Lovelock to pay a fine for exceeding a 45mph limit before leaving the city onwards to California.) This route is the vibrantly surviving mix of worldly hi-tech casinos, Micron's multi-million chip plant and high ideas flowing with Clarke's fellow Mormons. The late HBS Professor Clayton

Quadrant II: Illustrations 13-14
Hello Jumping Jackalope! Rock Springs, 6 June 1969

Christensen broke new ground with his idea of disruptive innovation; and Mitt Romney became 70th Governor of easterly Massachussetts in 2003, a presidential candidate in 2012 and a Senator from Utah in 2019.

Alexis De Tocqueville's writings *Democracy in America* in the 1800s are relived in the line that "America is great when it's good". Maybe Soong had chosen the uplifting northerly intuitive inspiration and avoided the parallel middle-Nevada 'ghostliest' Route 50 where the gold boom went bust and never recovered. I feel so highly favoured to see the future continuity of harsh arid and 'salt-lake' lands that sustain an unusual combo of humanists like Utah's Romney and Christiansen, Arizona's Goldwater and McCain, and Nevada's Reid and Sheldon whose religious, political cum business thought leadership hark back to De Tocqueville's times a hundred and fifty years ago!

4. *Farmer-Soldiers, Scholar-Warriors:* Our journey had started from New York, leaving my many West Point peerless and selfless warrior classmates whose 'line of grey' (officer's uniform) lost about half of their cohort fellow officers in the Vietnam War. Our continuing journey took us through Chicago where the 1968 Democrats' Convention saw the Anti-Vietnam War Protest resulting in shambles that led Nixon into fame and infamy. The farmer-soldiers of Montana of WWI were celebrated in the movie based on Jim Harrison's novel *Legends of the Fall* starring Anthony Hopkins and Brad Pitt. The experiences of WWII hero Audie Murphy were similarly depicted in a movie based on his book *To Hell and Back*. Likewise General

Eisenhower scholar-warrior or Ike (as in the movie *D-Day the Sixth of June* to retake Europe from Hitler). Travelling from Abilene in Texas to Kansas City (KC), Missouri, the Harry S. Truman Library and Museum remind us of President Truman who signed on the fateful atomic bombing on Hiroshima and Nagasaki that ended WWII. Fortuitously, KC is built upon the foresight of its favourite son Sinologist Edgar Snow, a friend of Chairman Mao Ze-Dong in the early 1930s, now perpetually endured by his named China Centre for Edgar Snow Studies, Peking University.

Warrior & Rocketry Redoubt: The mile-high Cheyenne atop the mountain heartland of Wyoming was so steep that even our BMW 2002 needed to engage the second gear. The hardened minuteman missile silos (from the 1776 America colonies' revolutionary minutemen) are depicted by the statue of Captain John Parker in the battle at Lexington Massachusetts. Paul Revere's ride to warn 'the British are coming' is likened to the global early warning system of NORAD, the North American Aerospace Defense Command located in the Cheyenne Mountain Complex. NORAD served to identify incoming Russian missiles (and tongue-in-cheek tracking Santa's sleigh at Christmas). That stirring revolutionary spirit is expressed in the anthem "The Star-Spangled Banner" that is still sung in every major sports event: "And the rockets' red glare, the bombs bursting in air, gave proof through the night that our flag was still there …" Revolution is not the monopoly of the Russians or Chinese. America was born in a revolution and good warrior-tradition. Remembering De Tocqueville's "America is great when it's good", after defeating Hitler and Tojo, America generously remade Europe and Japan after WWII through the magnanimity of the Marshall Plan. Let it not be forgotten and slip into basic slogans like "Make America Great Again" inadvertently pitting itself against unappreciated friends and courting rivals as in President Trump's version of America. Incidentally, there is a Chinese greeting, "May you live in interesting times"; it sounds like a good wish but it has a dark side to it, a delicate curse.

May the li'l warrior with the big heart still live on "dreading to leave an illiterate ministry to the churches" as warned in an old parchment record of Harvard's founders.

Respite: After the arduous climb up the 1,848-metre high Cheyenne upon crossing the Wyoming state line, we took a break at East Rock Springs

Quadrant II: Illustrations 15-17
Jackalope: Everpresent, Cowboy & Scouting Friendships

along Interstate I-80 at the El Rancho Motor Lodge on 6 June 1969. Owned by an enterprising and happy State Senator Louis Boschetto and well-run by the then Manageress Frances Anselmi, the El Rancho provided us with a well-earned respite to breathe the rare clean air, smell the roses and banter away (a pillow fight to a draw) with Soong and Frank. It was indeed so sweet to share friendships from an early age! El Rancho Motor Lodge is still featured on the Internet and is rated 4.5 out of 5!

In a mulling mood, I had flashes of thoughts as I contemplated the eerie height of America's contradiction. On the one hand, there was the brightening pursuit of happiness and on the other the darkly destructive every-ready nuclear armed minuteman missiles deep in the reinforced mountain rock. Such destructive arms were intended to keep the peace in the face of overwhelming mutual self-destruction if a nuclear war started with any leading adversary/ies.

The night sky of Cheyenne was azure with a billion stars – one ponders the wonders of being a minuscule single individual, yet always a unique one. Leaving behind the prairies and flocks of Robin Americaine (as the French Canadians call them) we move to the highlands, our pensive musings abetted at times with the possibility of hallucinating-induced effect of lesser oxygen. Indeed, I thought I saw the mythological 'Jackalope' of the 1800s. Like the half man half horse centaur, it is the half rabbit half antelope with deer-horns. But in a flash it disappears in speed or mirage. It never quite disappears as if bridges of the mind link the worlds of imagination and reality – a hybrid or is it an open-ended question? Maybe. Imagination ebbs and flows freely in the mid-hours of the twilight between the night and the early morning calm. It's a nice time to be writing this letter now, with breaks of WhatsApps and messages from my dear friends. From Vancouver, Patrick ("It's 2am in SG. Still counting sheep? Have a good night.") and in Singapore, Bull as in 'Chief Sitting Bull', extraordinary 85-year youngster Scout Master and fellow golfer ("It's 0500. Why so early? Going for golf?").

Into 2019, hybrids are common in daily life. There are hybrid-cars (run on petrol and/or electricity), hybrid golf clubs (combining the best features of iron-wood clubs from a sand-wedge to a No. 1-iron; and woods from a 7-wood to No. 1-wood driver). At the zoo, you can see the zonkey (black and white stripes like a zebra with the ears and 'stubbornness' of a donkey). And the list goes on as new technological breakthroughs in DNA and gene-splicing enable scientists to make a lot more creatures possible. Luckily such creations are subject to human and medical ethic rules and country laws. In Scotland, they cloned the first sheep named Dolly not by normal birth, but in the laboratory. Dolly has since died of "old age"!

UNBEKNOWNST 1

Scouting Links Wyoming, California & Senate: Although it is 50 years since that drive across America, this vignette has a nice contextual tale to it. As a UK Queen's Scout (Eagle Scout in America) driving through Wyoming to California one cannot miss the heart-warming story of Scout Norman Mineta (later California Congressman). In the 1940s he was placed in an internment camp for Japanese Americans. It was his Jamboree Visiting Scout Alan Simpson (later Wyoming Senator from Cody) who four decades after, jointly sponsored and passed the Civil Liberties Act of 1988, and an apology and reparations to Japanese Americans internees. Scouting friendship was the cornerstone to this bi-partisan collaboration, "I love that Scout Alan," said Norman as the scouting ditty goes:

"We have met in comradeship tonight,

Far across the deep blue seas (Pacific Ocean & Lake Akali by Cody, Wyoming),

Guide our golden memories,

And so before we close our eyes and sleep

Let us keep our hearts close and keep

Scouting friendship strong and deep

Till we meet again..."

We can revisit the case of the Mineta-Simpson scouting friendship and draw many additional takeaways by way of a time-out to replay and review our own thoughts or time with friends, too. The same can be done in probably about a dozen junctions throughout this letter by reviewing old photos and accessing websites like this one, about two boy scouts who met in an internment camp, grew up to work in Congress and remain as friends across a political divide.

 <https://www.theatlantic.com/family/archive/2019/05/congressmen-norm-mineta-alan-simpson-friendship-japanese-internment-camp/589603/>

UNBEKNOWNST 2

Once in a while in a pensive mood, I appreciate the blessing of the unbeknownst. And unbeknownst to me, Soong turns out to be the favourite Nephew of Madame Soong Meiling aka Madame Chiang Kaishek of the famous three Soong Sisters. Soong's Father was TL Soong whose grieving loss and obituary in the *New York Times* saluted a formidable life. In more sense than one, it was a private drive de force with Soong who later founded and managed Calistoga Spring & Geyser Company of Napa Valley. His colleagues to this day still celebrate his continuing legacy and generosity as a nuevo human being, entrepreneur, scholar and gentleman. Of his many cares, the love of his ailing whippet hound was touching (like Ulysses and his beloved Argo) as was his overseeing of the family-linked Bank of Canton, San Francisco. Later he went on a retreat at a monastery to reinvigorate in contemplation. For a fleeting week, I found a compleat renaissance man whilst riding across the vastness of America. His influence shaped my view of the depth of America's talent. In an osmotic way I drew inspiration from the life of Soong. Truth be told, we hardly had long conversations, but we communicated swimmingly well.

A bonus journey of discovery from sea to shining sea, my across America drive was a once in a lifetime experience with an episodic search of the idea of America from afar and near. The experience filled my abiding understanding of the girth, depth, warts and all of America, great yet complex. Recall President John Kennedy's bold 'dream far' youthfulness of 1961 to send a man to the moon (not because it's easy, but because it was hard) and return before the end of the 1960s. The first man on the moon, superhero Astronaut Neil Armstrong proclaimed "That's one small step for man, one giant leap for mankind" as he stepped onto the moon on 20 July 1969. That was many years after Jules Verne's great foresight in his 1865 novel *Journey from Earth to the Moon*.

Recalling also the mixed rainbows that straddled President Richard Nixon 1968 when he opened ties with China in 1972 (to balance-off Russia) compared to President Donald Trump 2016 when he started the first trade war 2018 with China (to re-balance for a fairer America-China trade). In effect, the higher tariffs created the unintended increase in costs to consumers and hurt the U.S. farmers badly. Just before you wonder why is it not Leo Soong and other renaissance Americans rising to the highest role of the land instead of Donald Trump, one should remember that Harvard in the first two decades of this 21st century gave us not one but two two-term Presidents, George W. Bush (2000-2008) hailing from the Business School and Barack Obama (2008-2016) from the Law School who also had the singular honour of being elected Editor of the *Harvard Law Journal*.

We may drive faster and farther, but it behoves us to respect the pendulum and rhythm of history. From *Jefferson-ian, Lincoln-ian to Jackson-ian*, thence to *Roosevelt-ian, Johnson-ian to Trump-ian*, has the pendulum now moved to normality *Biden-ian?* Sometimes these factors linger along longer and wobble the pendulum swing.

Quadrant III
Why Faster & Higher?

IN MY PRIVATE WORLD

Jun, I must hasten to thank Soong again, especially for helping me find myself. From my early hiking days covering a modest 30 miles at 3mph in the jungles of Malaysia, it was a 'Great Leap Forward' when I joined Soong driving farther at times 100mph through 3,000 'straight' miles across a continent in idea and reality, reaching seemingly unending far horizons spanning over twelve states of America! It wasn't a sprint, though the first six hundred miles dash to Toledo felt like it. It was, however, a marathon that gripped me for a week. In present 5G Internet times, I feel that the experience of the marathon has become interwoven into my life as a secondary (not at birth) total immersion in the River Styx of adventure, 'awe' and invulnerability.

Quadrant III: Illustrations 1-2
Driving I-80: 'River Styx' Immersion

To Soong, "Thank you for your generosity of heart, spirit and your masterly sense of time and space riding your sleek-blue cheetah BMW in perfect serenity along the Interstate 80 trail. May I be truly grateful. We both literally drove hard."

BREAKTHROUGH

From 800 Case Studies to the Real World: My sanity during the two years at boot camp Harvard Business School was sustained by the love of Swee Chee my dear fiancée, my dear youngest sister Mag who against all odds just after high school won the Miss Singapore 1968 title, and the indomitable Red Sox! The Red Sox were Boston's hallowed superhero fellow city-zens who in 1967 won the American Baseball League Championship. Jim Lonborg became the best pitcher and was honoured with the prestigious pitchers' Cy Young Award; in retirement he lived a happy life as a re-born successful dentist! Indeed, the 3,000-mile drive as co-driver and navigator with Soong was my benign breakthrough self-discovery 'road to Damascus moment' as apostle Paul described it. The drive was a return to the real world. It evoked the transforming takeaway, a transitioning from the daily grind of wrestling with 800 case-studies during the two-year MBA programme to sharpen and hone our knowledge and skills to drive our eventual chosen business(es). You've got to actually drive!!!

It was a precious week of absorption and reflection of everything that is America. It was also a time of reflection about myself. Because in life we have to take time to think and sometimes 'think about the unthinkable' (as the Hudson Institute's best-known futurist thinker Herman Kahn would say). A time of reflection is a time to be strategic, nuevo and capture the spirit and unapparent mega-trends of the times and ourselves! In investment terms it's about 'free time flow' for thinking (like uncommitted free cash flow that you could invest in better things or deals).

Route I-80 was for me a once in a lifetime 3,000-mile adventure. Was it driven by plain or true curiosity? I continue to think about it. In the final segment through the desert from the fine salt lakes to San Francisco, we got caught up in the real world when the cross winds threatened to sweep us off the sandy, treeless and bleak Nevada desert road. Our unease was visual! The VW Beetle in front of us was swaying left to right and back again! For if you ever get stuck in the sand, you have only the heat, time and hope that a friendly motorist driving an equivalent of an SUV or a Ford Truck with a tow line would rescue you. Otherwise, you face the uncertain wait for the tow-truck hollered from the next big town or service centre. Safe from the desert sands, we took an acute turn onto a narrower 'blue highway' at higher than Goldilocks' speed. All at once the

Quadrant III: Why Faster & Higher? 49

Quadrant III: Illustrations 3-4
Venturing out to Unknown Territories and Terrains

Quadrant III: Illustrations 5-6
Escape Hatch to Cheyenne's Clouds

unexpected epiphany happened! Happily early training in the Outward Bound School and hiking through unknown terrains unexpectedly activates a safety-catch. A higher sense of the experience kicks in as if in slow-motion as you silently talk your way into guiding the car to the tight runway of the adjoining, thankfully, traffic free road. And it was surreal at the same time. Your whole life is unwound as if in a slow-motion movie!

Back to the real world to the last syllable of planning, all final arrangements were targeted to fall into place: you've to manage time, place, return flight to Boston for Commencement; and return home to SG without running out of cash or missing flights. (Those were the days when fewer alternative flights existed.)

From Case Studies to Driving: You need to actually apply knowledge, skills and attitudes in learning to drive. Half-way across the world during my 2015 Golf Tournament, the pathos of distance brought together the inter-inspiration between YY and Uncle Yun that was driving us to achieve 1st and 3rd places. As I rode with Soong 3,000 miles across America on Route I-80, I searched to think whether I had deep-learnt anything from 45 years ago. I know he made me realise my inner-self (as different from myself) more profoundly than two-years of class-experience dissecting 800 real-life cases. But my everlasting self-learning is that you can learn all about learning and acquiring skill, knowledge and attitude of any discipline or driving (a car or your golf tee-off) for that matter. But the magic of the mix is you must actually drive, you must actually do it! Drive Soong did – the first six hundred miles from New York City to Toledo Ohio in about 10 to 12 hours including meal breaks, tough as nails but making it look like a cake walk! I have only once on the short NYC-Niagara return ever driven as a sole easy-rider on the interstate with no retracing and definitely no retreat. Always driving forward, without turning back, you begin to realise what unrelenting driving commitment over 3,000 miles is like, with still miles to go before you sleep. It turns out to be a joy! Drive I did, too, as a standby when Soong and our pre-med advised, which I was most happy to do! Thanks to Soong for letting me ride his favourite steed after sitting twin-riding. But as true cowboys Soong and Frank never swapped their auto-steeds – Man and horse are one and inseparable just as the Lone Ranger (in a series created by radio studio WXYZ Detroit) rides his beloved 'Hi-Yo Silver' (a white stallion) and no one else. We both drove hard, joyously with a lovely sense of arrival at the Pacific, a lake to Asia!

MILES & ROADS

For me, the journey presented the rhythm and transformative gifts of the challenges of the earlier 5 miles, 10, 20, 30, 100, 1,000 to the far horizon(s) of 3,000 miles to the high Sierras and the cauldron of ever-changing California, another facet of emerging new America of the future. What was the common factor? It is that whatever challenges these miles and roads threw at us, we dealt with them, survived and overcame them, even when near disaster struck whilst transversing the Nevada desert! At another level, the journey presented so much coincidence with a common theme and coherence of a healthy spreading chestnut tree of life, network and inter-generational connections. There are linkages from my early cub-scouting days dealing with seniors, peers and juniors and the evolving armature of the past-ure (past-linked future). For example, a happy pal to this day from way back then, is Uncle Chuan Lock who in happenstance, was married the same year in 1969, has 2 girls and 1 boy (me, 3 boys) who married and blessed us with six grandchildren each; and we jointly celebrated our 50th wedding anniversary in 2019.

IMAGINEERING YOUR LIFE & DREAMS

But I did miss out on a few things, as intuitively forward, I was wrapped up in starting work, a new life with my sweetheart and starting a family. Time flew by. Three children and six grandchildren later, I now write this letter to you, my eldest grandson, Jun.

Let me now revisit those providential experiences and how I found myself hiking. I restarted life in Singapore on about S$15,000 annually and worked unceasingly hard in the hope that my life would not be trapped by the potential revenge of the pledge of poverty in the founding Divinity School which Harvard was committed to in 1636. I paid off my $1,500 loan. In faith, life panned out and thankfully, reality eventually matched the narrative of miles and challenges of distances. It was a surreal mix just as my social philosopher-crooner Dean Martin shared in his song 'That's Amore' with the magical line "When you walk in a dream, but you know you're not dreaming". That's good enough for me because it's strange but real, you know! The future might yield a radical thinking at the intersection of quantum physics with quantum psychology creating a new reality. That's too deep for me.

Quadrant III: Illustrations 7-8
Blue Moon above Clouds on High

But to know more about the fusion of breakthrough science and spirituality, you could refer to Valerie Varan's book *Living in a Quantum Reality: Using Quantum Physics and Psychology to Embrace Your Higher Consciousness* at <https://www.amazon.com/gp/aw/s//ref=mw_dp_a_s?ie=UTF8&i=books&k=Valerie+Varan>.

I would simply celebrate the 'dream' idea of Dean Martin. With some degree of the romance of life, I had travelled west from SG to HBS, finding the deepest recesses of myself driving west from New York to San Francisco! When you visited Disneyland in Tokyo and HK, Jun, you were able to appreciate the world of imagination and curiosity of the future brought alive by the Queen of Hearts in Alice in Wonderland, Winnie the Pooh, Space Mountain and Star Trek. Walking in the weave of the dream world is a process that coined the idea of 'imagineering'. At Disneyland there is total devotion to a make-believe customer experience. Disney staff never chit-chat with each other as the Disney imagination must be free flowing, not broken up – unlike at a supermarket when cashiers talk and shout at each other in front of customers who simply need good service and often don't get it. For Disney it's the bio-sphere, the total sensation of imagination and Foxy's thinking word of 'however' versus the status quo word of 'moreover'.

The joy of life is to always seek, discover and create and not fear the unknown. Friendships are a treasure. The ideas and networks that you create and invest in have pleasing benefits for a happy and richer joy of life or *joie de la vie* in French. You would not believe that I found another set of the three volumes *The Discoverers, The Creators and The Seekers* by Daniel Boorstin, former Librarian of the United States Congress. It was such serendipity to discover them in Raven's Used Bookstore on the old Church Street by Harvard Square in May 2019. My life-long naturalist, banker, scholar, benefactor (of libraries), philanthropist and a man for all seasons Dr Lee Seng Tee was keen on this trilogy which I presented to him as a belated 95th birthday gift. *The Discoverers* has a connected subtext to this letter – common to all of us is the search to understand our world and know ourselves.

I had given an earlier gift of the eight-volume Everyman 19th Century Edition of Richard Hakluyt's *The Principal Navigations, Voyages, Traffiques and Discoveries of the English Nation* to Dr Lee who had in turn gifted it to Harvard's Widener Library. It was exquisitely bound in a green cloth-clad cover with gilded edging. I had purchased it from antiquarian Sarah Key's The

Quadrant III: Illustration 9
Imagineering your Life & Dreams

Haunted Bookshop at St Edward's Passage, Cambridge UK. In this connection, I am reminded of the HBS 25th Anniversary Colloquium incorporating societal elements in graduate business education which I am highly invested in. The power of parallel informal networks can be found in Attachment I – Emailed Letter Excerpts from Boston ~ July'81, April'97, June'04 to May'19. In these excerpts I cite my 40-year labour of love in diverse and deep global alumni-ae and self-educating colloquia in co-leadership with HBS Senior Associate Dean for International Affairs, Professor Warren McFarlan.

THE QUESTION REMAINS

Why do you do it again and again? Is it for the more important self-learning 'process and the learning about yourself' and the beauty and nuances of the world we live in? Management guru Gary Hamel's strategic view of the future similarly accents process rather than product in an unending journey of the future(s). So did Samurai Musashi (not just by winning duels but by defeating your yesterday's self then assert yourself with the rest of your fellowmen). Similarly the 500-year Society of Jesus Jesuit Priests were dedicated to continual self-reflection, improvement and transformation. Who would have thought that praying the Lord's Prayer for a thousand years since the gospels were written that the first ever Jesuit Pope Francis I could ever think to revise the doctrinal tenet 'and lead us not into temptation but deliver us from evil' (Latin: *Et ne nos inducas in tentationem, sed libera nos a malo*) into the reinvigorating faith to intercede for strength to overcome temptation!

Like most Singaporeans at the time, YY was born in Singapore's Kandang Kerbau (literally translates to a "buffalo cage" in the Malay language) Hospital aka KK. But like few Singaporeans, I was raised on a farm in Malaya's rural Endau near Johore's Rompin during WWII before moving back to Singapore to a farm at the original Frankel Estate. Growing up on a farm gave me an advantage on fundamental vanilla reality. I was carrier of water and hewer of wood. Indeed YY was the champion two-some with the long axe severing into two a 9-inch diameter thick 3-foot coconut-trunk in about 12 seconds at the 1960s Stamford Scouts' District Games. You would also notice I possess an axe-like hard-hitting chopping iron-golf swing. In farming you nurture lives – the raising of pigs, chickens, ducks and geese. You also have to clear new land and plant by the season be it in monsoon, thunder, rain or sun. There was the constant race to catch the season. If I didn't know what to do, my Mom, Eldest Sister and Brother would remind me.

MULTI-MILLION DOLLAR SOCIAL ENTERPRISE

Faster ~ completed in 15 months instead of 18 months. *Bigger* at $100 million but at cost-effective $85 million.

In my mind's eye I visualised the enormity of the social impact of Singapore being the venue of the first and pioneering Youth Olympic Games or YOG 2010. It was the first International Olympic Committee-sanctioned event held in Singapore. I was put in charge of converting (major renovations with a few complementary buildings) the 200-hectare Campus of the Nanyang Technological University (NTU) into the YOG-NTU Games Village. The Games Village was to accommodate 5,000 athletes (of university seeking age) and officials from 200 global IOC Member countries. I had to oversee the conversion of the campus within 18 months whilst simultaneously performing my normal daily Troika management duties, and as COO overseeing half a dozen divisions, serving with the President, the Provost I accepted NTU President's appointment upon his commission but this time it was with a tinge of educated enthusiasm. I knew I could do it, but I had to figure it all out. My educated enthusiasm as distinct from unreserved spontaneity reminded me of the 2000 Sydney Olympics where my alumnus pal Nick Greiner'70 was central to its success. (I last met up with him in 1997 when I also interviewed his Vietnam Veteran Deputy PM Tim Fischer and urbane Foreign Secretary Alexander Downer for an article on the emerging new Australia which Tim called 'Maxi-Tiger' instead of 'Asia's Rising Tiger Economies'). The IOC has had oversight of a score of Olympic Games Villages in the past hundred years. All in all, it was a practical Schumpeterian thought that the mission was to be a vocational adaptation, not the higher order of a nuovo innovation.

MAJOR MISSIONS & MINOR MISSIONS

It's easier to be clear about the major mission – but more importantly are the key mini missions. In consultation with IOC Field Chief Albert Felli to yield his unshared 'secret milestones', it turns out that there are 640 milestones in the IOC Games Village Specs & Ops. Put simply – with the time-tested milestones of prior Olympic Games Villages, my undivided will was that it could (and would) be completed according to specifications and on time. What I brought to this project team was age and experience to see the way ahead, armed with all that I could muster by way of inspiration, enthusiasm and my hands-on oversight as head of Campus Office FPM (Facilities, Planning & Management). Coincidentally, I had always been impressed with the Olympian Spirit, Grace of Champions and Olympians. In my own almost foolhardy way, I thought I was prepared for the task having completed 3,000 miles and more, with added worldly experience. It was an SG national project. Failure was not an option. Being in charge means always being under pressure to 'defeat any problem' (missile-scientist President Kalam's advice and proven needed attitude), to keep the team focused, safe and free from the university's administrative powerful executives who might be wont to advise and interfere. In truth, it's like creating a distinctive bio-sphere free from outside unsolicited advice and interferences. Thankfully there was a confluence as a ruling member of the Troika with

Quadrant III: Why Faster & Higher?   57

Quadrant III: Illustration 10
Long Cloud 9~Darwin's Thinking Path?

Quadrant III: Illustration 11
Full Faith Plunge into Unknowns: Creating YOG Games Village'10

Quadrant III: Illustrations 12-15
Houston, We've Company!

also the responsibility for Board relations, on behalf of and with the team, we were able to gain credibility with the key internal and external stakeholders in NTU, and the IOC YOG Games Executive Commission headed by Ukrainian Sergey Bubka pole-vault Olympic Gold Medallist. Stakeholders included SG's YOG-IOC, Ministry of Culture, Community and Youth, Ministry of Education, Ministry of Finance, and officials from IOC Geneva.

It takes a good Olympic Games Village to enable the Olympic values to shine through. Additionally, it takes an eco-system of shared home village values, practice and encouragement to go for Olympic Gold. It is the Villages and the daily run over the Trelawny Hills of Jamaica that made the faster, gazelle-like graceful and unbeatable sprinter Husain Bolt'08; the barrios of Cuba that made the earlier 400 and 800-metre precursor Alberto Juntorena'76; the Ugandan Serengeti where 400-metre hurdler John Akebua'72 ran at such sprint speeds with zebras in order to catch their tails; the highland Kenyan Kijiji (villages is Swahili) tending goats (smarter sons take care of asset management) and running the hilly terrain that made miler Kip Keino'68; and the village policeman marathoner Abebe'60 who ran barefooted in the Ethiopian mountains and again on the roads in Rome. And of course there was the 'first Husain Bolt', the tall, fair and handsome Gold Medal Olympian'76 Alberto Juntorena (later Sports Minister) of Cuba's unbeatable fluid locomotion in the 400 and 800-metre 'dash' that left everyone behind in his wake.

During a visit by the Olympian IOC President Dr Jacques Rogge (Orthopaedic surgeon and sailor) in the preparatory stages of the YOG, he engaged with 300 youthful NTU graduates from some 100 countries including two well-spoken Kazakhstan lady graduates (with computer science specialty) who set the enthusiastic tone and quality of the discourse in an interview for the NTU Newsletter. See <https://www3.ntu.edu.sg/ yov/articles/article_MyPaper_100324_A19_Roggeeagertowitnessfun-filledYOG.pdf>.

Jun, you learnt from your Maths at Kumon, calculating fractions, margins and return on investing (on the incremental extra time and effort). The return on investment or ROI of NTU inheriting the $100 million assets from YOG Games Village was generously conferred on NTU in exchange for about $30 million of additional sweat exceeding the exacting investors' expectation of a hurdle rate of 25%! That's why the price of success is hard, hard work by co-sweating leadership. We do it together while leaders we trust *'see'* the way to do it. (A side reading with details can be found in Attachment II that shows your learnt 'Kumon-type' calculation.)

- If I may take a moment, I will briefly touch on the fun and play of visualisation. As a young schoolboy walking home instead of taking the bus, visuals are replayed in my mind from seeing sets of double: confirming main and minor landmarks to activities on a map of the route. When you first realise it, there is a strange feeling especially when the images come in 'frame by frame'. It's kind of nice to 'play visualising', as results turn up nicely, are enjoyable and intuitively hone that visualisation as a skill.

How so, Jun? Life during those days was more basic and naturally simpler, there were no readily available land-line telephones, definitely no mobile devices or iPhones with its eyeball-catching screen addiction.

The connected landmarks of what I saw on my walk home as a schoolboy were a bridge, boats, unloading-loading, stevedores, warehouses and shops. These are all part of the living 'place-making' of the riverine entrepôt trade of rice, people, business, and the microcosm of the regional-global link to the Singapore port and the world.

Crossing the bridge at New Bridge Road by the then Hill Street Police Station (now converted into a better social ID of the upmarket happening Clarke Quay), you could see the 'tongkangs', with their two painted 'spirit eyes' to ward off bad stuff. There were also the sun-burnt sweating stevedores hard at work hauling 50-kg sacks of rice on their backs using a leather back-piece linked to a forehead strap and walking the bouncy single gang-plank to the quayside warehouses. They were aided by a baling cargo hook (à la 'Captain Hook') to create an OMO (one man operation) by using the hook to lift the sack, keep it in place and unload onto a walk-up sack hill of rice sacks. There were no forklift trucks, only brawn, sweat and grit. As a senior scout, I was able to translate that OMO by carrying a layer at a time (you need two to pitch a tent for ten occupants) from the lorry to the campsite.

Past the bridge were the towkay rice merchants in their silky '555' T-shirt singlets and dark pantaloons; shopkeepers wore the 'Chilli' or 'Swan' brand T-shirts and short pants. Later I discovered that the T-shirts said a lot: Hong Kong made '555' shirt-wearer shops filled the wealthier Carpenter and Hong Kong streets (where Robert Kuok of sugar and rice fame had his original lucky offices). The ordinary mini-marts (with all manner of goods jam packed displayed and dangled from roofs) of those days along the terrace-unit shops were more modest with their China-made whites. Their money-till was conspicuously a pre-used biscuit tin hung with a counter-balance weight for the frugal, visual but defining accounting, conservatively showing that 'Cash is King'.

Fast forward 50 years and lots of hard work, those early merchants and their succeeding two school-going generations are now among SG's 250,000 multi-millionaires – whose terrace shophouses are each valued at about $5–$10 million.

On the other side of the river, is Tew Chew Street where the wet Ellenborough Market was (now Central Building adjacent to Traders/Jen Hotel) by the old Wayang Street (there was a semi-permanent wayang stage, now Merchant Street). The big deal? It's the go-to 'sure cure' traditional Chinese Medical Hall which looks like a welcoming temple – styled in 'Southern Chinese secular architecture', the exemplary Thong Chai Medical Institution of 1867 (it's now at Chin Chew Street opposite Manhattan House). My Mother and friends patronised it. The orangey ('kum-kum' as in Cantonese) and bitter taste of herbal medicine is long lasting, and my healthful autumn-winter years prove these to have worked well, even then in episodic ways. The bigger deal is the big-idea – the Sinic Confucianist teaching of social responsibility that with success comes the need to care for your fellowmen and the community.

This little hike home, innocuous as it was, added a lasting impact – 'To do a little good as you're passing through is what the Lord would have us do'. This I had gregariously learnt from my scouting and comrades on our little hikes and big hikes that are founded on core values of the Scout's Honour, Duty and Promise. *"On my honour I will do my best to do my duty to God and my country and to obey the Scout Law; to help other people at all times, to keep myself physically strong, mentally awake, and morally straight."* And of course, the moniker of 'Be prepared' – striving lifelong to always be, learning always when sometimes, not.

Serendipitously, in December 2019, I was in Central Building by Tew Chew Street with my dear colleague Keen Whye for a social capital development meeting with the NVPC (National Volunteer & Philanthropy

Centre) in sharing its mission for 'The City of Good'. Together with other mission-minded individuals we endowed a scholarship programme in perpetuity to HBS' advanced management programme. The scholarship provides added capacity development of chief executives for the not-for-profit sector who continue their wondrous works to care for our fellow-men and the community. They are folks like our pioneer scholar a dozen years ago medical Dr CC Ow who now is CEO of the expanding and integrated-care centennial Kwong Wai Shiu Hospital. Five years ago, he was joined by Dr Goh Wei-Leong, founder of HealthServe to help individuals in medical need; he also provided exemplary anti-Covid service for our foreign workers who were staying in dormitories.

Hiking and visualising with mission-mindfulness can be envisioned more neatly in project-oriented missions. One such example is the *first and faster* 9-month project (not unusual to need 12 months) to produce the Champion Winner at the 38th Chingay Procession, a Singapore tradition held annually during Chinese New Year. It was NTU's float of three fire-breathing dragons, Draconika of 2009, that profiled visually the engineering, technology and artistic rendition of three independently 'robotic' moving fire-resistant dragons and 120 dancers.

The engineering and technology parts were tough enough. When things go wrong, they just do! On the grand opening day reviewed by our dragon-year born Prime Minister Lee Hsien Loong, the robotic young NTU dragon was reluctant to move! So my expert faculty Professor Gerald Seet spontaneously jumped onto the float, laid down beside it and thankfully coaxed it to perform by tech and prayer, thus saving all of us from public dismay which may have needed us to flee to the hills with lowing heads.

The higher order sub-theme was subtle and more difficult to portray ~ we are no Philistine warriors and engineers! After all the choreography, rehearsals and pep-talks, the real McCoy was for me a jolting epic extravaganza when it all came together in living colour setting the new gold standard for any institution to match and exceed. The NTU Student Union President Ms Ng was 'filled with pride'. Justly so, as Draconika was created with lots of enthusiasm and love by faculty, graduates and staff volunteers in a seemingly impossible 9-month window whilst performing our regular daily duties. You can view the Draconika parade on YouTube at: <https://youtu.be/y1Z_Mqd7-G4>.

As mentioned above, another example of visualisation of a mission that is *faster & bigger* is the 18-month (done in 15 months) $100 million project to convert NTU Campus into the secure, renovated and built Inaugural Youth Olympic Games Village (YOGV) ahead of time and below budget whilst exceeding specified global standards for IOC Olympic Games Villages.

Without serial visualisation and unwavering support for the hands-on project leadership it would not have been possible to infuse confidence, action and faith with such a quantum fount of heart-spirit (as in Entheos). The project team completed a never ever tried multi-million project whilst doing our normal daily duties in administrating a 35,000-student university. Unwavering 'hands-on leadership' is how strategist Sima Yi led his officers and troops who refused to leave him despite his personal error in occupying the enemy vacated fort, a trap set for him with delayed exploding booby-traps causing widespread fires. They stayed and fought side by side with him and were willing to die with him to overcome Zhuge Liang at the final battle. But the heavens favoured Sima Yi and with good fortune, heavy rains came to stanch the fires. Sima Yi finally overthrew the Cao Dynasty and established his Jin Dynasty. Years later, there was a repeat performance of his loyal officers and troops rallying to him fast, indeed in a speeded up version of faster, in an accelerated and decisive battle. Sima Yi was facing advancing age and sudden involuntary early retirement from his Military Command on that fateful Qing Ming Day when the Emperor and his Royal Entourage left the walled Capital of the Empire to perform their annual solemn homage to their ancestors. This time, by a comprehensive and unexpected swifter assembling of an overwhelming force, it was with great precision, not luck, that he succeeded completely.

As a backdrop of our lives, there exists preserved in our mind, the faith of our fathers as a perpetual source of inspiration. A picture-perfect illustration is the photograph of our beloved late Minister Mentor Lee Kuan Yew declaring shortly after separation from Malaysia in 1965 with his classic roaring raw rhetoric, a rich vision for Singapore within a faster decade (not multi-decade). It was the vision that in ten years there would be a thriving metropolis. He not only achieved that vision but exceeded it beyond compare! He brought us from Third World to First!

As the nominal leader of both NTU projects, the Youth Olympic Village in 2010 and the Chingay Float in 2009 I'm no engineer. An optimist am

I, with an urge for being an enthusiast-ser, visualiser and mission-minded sherpa. I took on the responsibility, fearlessly as Musashi dictated. I was committed to it as vouched by my words to the NTU President, that I would cut off my head and present it to him if I failed (as in the *Romance of the Three Kingdoms*). It's scary to say so. But with my assembled and faithful team, I could visualise those stages of completion, decelerating or accelerating. Inshallah (The Lord, permitting), all came to a good conclusion.

Later in life my Social Science professor pals tell me that's what ethnographic research is all about—observation, visualisation, analysis and when everything comes together, 'flow' is experienced, however fleeting.

Back to the narrative. It's amazing, Jun, that once you overcome the *fear of fear*, things become easier whether they be problems, untried options or crises.

Quadrant III: Illustration 16
Heli-View: Hi-lander Hyperboreans & Lo-lander Ulysses-eans

Quadrant III: Illustration 17
My Guardian Angel?

The word "crisis" in Chinese possesses both danger and opportunity.

The basic question comes back: why do you want to do it and higher?

The most novel reply I learnt was 'Nietzsche made me do it' in a *New York Times* Opinion column on 22 September 2018 by J. Kaag who authored the book *Hiking with Nietzsche: On Becoming Who You Are*.

It's the philosophy of stretching yourself, setting (higher) ambitious goals, creating the 'bandwidth of your inner spirit' (to which I would add sinews and robustness) or as Nietzsche says the 'pathos of distance'. I take that to imply multi-directions of distance, height, breadth and depth in overcoming your old self; and in the simplest Confucianist resolution, it's a journey of a thousand miles that starts with one bold step.

Here, you may understand it more easily if I set it in Greek mythology which you're reading more deeply (like my godson Gavin Ng at your age). It's about the hyperboreans who are the warriors of the higher mountains. They are somewhat like the Amazons though hyperboreans are men and women. They exist in high and higher peaks closer to the gods and heavens but in the tough cold cold north. Hyperboreans are in sync with extremes—extreme cold, tough-mindedness, overcoming odds, gigantic size (10-foot tall) and youthfulness (1,000-year lives). Absolutely, no fear of heights. So like Mallory, when asked why he wanted to climb that mountain, he said, "Because it's there!"

To make a rough and ready real life connection by association hyperborean qualities can be seen in the 1953 conquerors of the rarefied highest 8,848-metre Mount Everest. As a student in Primary 3 and an avid reader of the daily *Straits Times,* I recall how Nepalese Sherpa Norgay Tenzing who in the moment of suddenance, instinctively impaled Sir Edmund Hillary's repel rope and restrained it firmly onto the icy rock, saving him from meeting the jagged crevasse of the floor below.

Or the Olympians who in 1968 at the higher 2,250-metre Mexico City broke world records like hyperboreans such as Kenyan runner Kip Keino's 1,500-metre gold medal. Or American Bob Beamon who trained at mile-high Denver to a long jump flying past the magical 29-foot barrier (remaining as the Olympic Record today). And fellow athlete civil engineer Dick Fosbury who invented the reverse high jump levitating past 2.22 metres, higher than the new unknowns of human high jumping. Not forgetting the earlier hyperborean from the 2,355-metre Addis Ababa Abebe Bikila who won Gold running barefooted in the 1960 Rome Olympics, like the descendants of King Memnon of the 'Ethiopians and conqueror of the East' who fought in the Greco-Trojan War as allies of Troy's King Priam. And with great admiration I recall also the orthopaedic surgeon Dr Jacques Rogge from Belgium's Ghent by the River Lys who competed in sailing, lived in and served as IOC high official inspecting Olympic Villages for the next forty years right up to the Beijing Olympics of '080808' and who said of the YOG-NTU Games Village 2010, "This is amongst the best!"

Why are they special? In Kaag's words: Hyperboreans are giants who live "beyond the north wind", higher in unforgiving mountains, perfectly happy in seemingly unbearable conditions. The Greek poet Pindar said that "neither disease nor bitter old age is mixed in their sacred blood". They take inordinate risks but live to a thousand years!

Alas, I hiked for hours, days, accumulated months and strong hiking-built-in shin muscles (like the oriental chef with a visible 'wok muscle' between the thumb and index finger from hours of stirring the wok and creating nouvelle cuisine!). Fortune smiled on me in many of life's challenges. But I don't do extreme sports like Alex Honnold (or Tommy Caldwell who autographed his book *Push* for me) best known for his free-solo climbing, without safety equipment or ropes, of the higher <u>and</u> extreme 3,000-foot El Capitan sheer cliff face in Yosemite National Park in 2017. The documentary Free Solo won an Oscar in 2019: video clips are available at <https://m.youtube.com/watch?v=urRVZ4SW7WU>.

Found in the low lands and rolling hills, streams, rivers and the sea, hiking and wandering to find yourself are challenged by 'higher and noble goals' as Nietzsche might wish. But for me, I share the human sensibilities of a Greek Odysseus-ean or a Roman Ulysses-ean.

Quadrant IV
Enthusiasm, Faster & Forever

Dear Jun, to conclude this letter I've indelible memories of your fearlessness that are 'seared in my hippocampus'. We were taking part in the Grandpa-Grandson golf tourney (you were then about 4 years old) at the National Service Resort Golf & Country Club (Changi). You were aiming to get out of the deep 7-foot bunker (twice your height) by the Par 3 green for the first time ever. On the spur of the moment my advice for you was to do exactly what you usually do but that you must 'finish' your swing with your pitching wedge. And we won the Runner-Up Prize!

Marshalling your skill and will to match the challenge and cancel the opponent's offence – this is more than fearlessness. You displayed such an amazing performance winning the Junior 2018 Floorball Tourney by your awe-inspiring instinctive high foot-kick to prevent your opponent's gleeful expected goal-in score (a format of 3 on 3 with no goalie to defend the goal-net). You instilled in your team the curious calm whenever you were the goalie (or an acrobatic anti-goal high kick!) That's a capability to create a quantum sensation of intergalactic dynamic curved spacetime 'gravity waves' of 2017 as opposed to simpler or linear static mechanics of Newton's up and down law of gravity of 1687. Your skill in floorball displayed no uncertainty while *visualising in the mind's eye a 'Kodak-moment' of a winning save with foot not hands!* Remember what you said in your own words and drawing titled "Legendary".

Your school's SJIJ Excellence Award 2018 for an outstanding contribution in Floorball on Friday, 5 April 2019 is added evidence of your forever inspiration and implied trajectory (also the winning team of Season 2019). Life is not always so straightforward because it's transitioning to a quantum mix of uncertainty (not a linear extrapolation) and you have to react accordingly so. But you are along the right path; and spot on to credit Captain Karl, teammates, teacher-coaches, parents, supporters and league competitors for their fighting spirit and good cheer, win or lose.

Barriers Versus Reality: In 1986, six-year old Cody Sheehy of Wallowa County in Oregon got lost. Yet he found his way back after an 18-hour trek of 15 to 20 miles over mountains. So, my 30-mile Perak trek in 9 hours with a well-trained adult team wasn't such a big deal in context! Later, at the age of about 40, Sheehy became a Tucson-based successful documentary film-maker and sailor, drawing on his experience. "As a little kid, I had this opportunity to be tested and learn that there really aren't any barriers. I think a lot of people figure that out. They just might not figure it out at six." Cody Sheehy profiles the early enthusiasm and its lasting impact on his life of creativity and wanderlust forever!

Cody decisively learnt breaking the fear barrier. I daresay for others including me, we must be conscious to upgrade ourselves to be a better model (just like 3G to 4G to 5G to $n^{th}G$), strengthen our inner-self and not let fear creep back in stealth.

Quadrant IV: Illustration 1

We're not Alone~Oregonian Cody Aces GPS Test at 6

Early Major & Minor Missions: Another way of thinking that there aren't any barriers (everyone can indeed breach the word barrier or hurdle), reminds me when in Grade V (at age 11), my class teacher, the *'ibenesque'* drama of ideas, Mr Goon asked who would volunteer to read *The Count of Monte Cristo* by Alexandre Dumas after he regaled us over a few weeks as an incentive for being well-behaved. At stake was the honour of my class and classmates. So I raised my hand to volunteer to read the book – it turned out to be a 1,300-page novel with over 450,000 words! I loved reading and had been speed-reading the newspapers every day since Grade 1 as I was the daily newspaper buyer. Mr Goon was generous – he allowed me 2 weeks to finish reading the book. So, I broke it into mini missions – about 130,000 words a day or 100 pages spread over four hours a day (two on the daily bus trip and two at home in the afternoon). To make it more interesting to myself, I developed my own style of 'symmetric reading': a beginning chapter and a matching ending chapter, concluding in the middle of the novel; and then zipping through from front to end to retest the flow and dynamics. Alas, I took a dozen days, some hazing and two days to gel my thoughts with a crisp 4-point bulletin:

1. The story parallels Mr Goon's telling (*Mr Goon smiled at the credit*).

2. The tale is very dark, about Dantes' enemies, the vengeful inspector, the desolation and despair of imprisonment and Dantes' darkness as he was consumed by vengeance (*O dear!*)

3. The saving grace is the lovely Mercedes (not our classmate Chuan Lock Father's blue Mercedes Benz, laughter) and her unconditional love for Dantes (*classmates' giggles*)

4. But in all this darkness was Dumas' mastery in painting the light at the end of the tunnel – **Azure sky**. Not Royal Blue, not Cambridge Blue but lapis blue of the **exotic Afghan-Persian 'lapis lazuli'** – Latin for stone, heaven & skies. (*Gasp! Wow! And the transient 15-minute fame.*)

… 'saw a blue sea and azure sky.'

… 'of Monte Cristo, reddened by the burning sun, was seen against the azure sky.'

I am pleased to say, like Cody I did not regress back to the word barrier; and I did not have to break this Word Barrier again. Fear is different, it has an innate feature in the human being or psyche. You could fall back if you are not careful.

So, Jun, at the age of 4 you achieved a clean shot out of the 7-foot golf course bunker with a pitching-wedge onto the putting green. At the age of 12, your Dad Kwan got his diverse UK classmates out of the foggy treeless moors when he was at Sherborne Prep School in about 1984. I felt he had an in-built GPS and over the years more evidence bore this out. At 16, on his first ten provisional golf-rounds for submission of cards to gain his handicap, with a similar pitching-wedge, your Dad landed the ball on the green 160 yards away just beyond a pond. He understood his strength and skill to lower the club angle to mimic a 7-iron and later went on to win the longest drive novelty prize at 300 yards using an old Taylor Made Persimmon Wood. His strategy disoriented our third player, a mid-handicapper, who changed from his 7-iron choice to a 9-iron and his ball found the pond! At 22, your Dad was the Parade Commander (with the natural Arabic aura of 'hayba' of command) of his graduating Officer Cadet School Class'94 where the then PM's son was in the graduating Officer Medical Corps. And your late Auntie Kim, just then out of high school, without fear entered the beauty pageant, against many a naysayer, and was crowned Miss Singapore 1968. *Fearlessness is possible at a young age.* The elder generations may not have the monopoly to inspire. At twelve you make me want to better myself after our practice game where you outdrove me at 180 metres with a 3-hybrid versus my driver. Your skillset had won you second placing in an earlier tournament. Two things stand out in your ability to visualise and execute: winning the Mandai Course's daily challenge at the 160-metre first Par 3 with your 5-iron landing within 5.5 metres and your pre-announced and intended 100-metre 'draw' shot curving right around the palm tree and successfully landing on the green. The added feature is your ability to visualise yourself doing the shot and sussing the outcome versus the effort and importantly gauging what's the gap to address.

I am inspired by your work ethic and commitment on the journey to create and hone the elusive combo of skill and will, of overcoming the challenge in practice and at the most important time of the real competition. Success is elusive as you have to figure it out as you go along like 'rongorongo'. Try deciphering the hieroglyphic of the Easter Islands whilst visiting the huge stone statues before going to the Galapagos Island made famous by Darwin on his way to publishing his five most important words 'The Survival of the Fittest'.

That's the easy part. The tough part in golf is to figure out when in the repository of angle mastery, your skill matches the challenge. As the golfing champions say, the 'zone' sets in and you overcome all things with flow and fluidity to win even if a 'minor' tension slips in here and there, but you prevail. Nevertheless, be humble and ever-learning and avoid being seduced by the desk-bound scholar's illusion of mastery.

Jun, you now have the advantage of happily pursuing two-track success, that is doing well in the dreaded parents' annual sixth-year worry of the Primary School Leaving Examination or PSLE and winning in your golfing

Quadrant IV: Illustrations 2-3
Where Have all the Birds Gone? Pre-modern Drones, Ravens

Quadrant IV: Illustration 4

Imagine SG vs. Egypt (Giza Pyramids)

competitions. Success is easy to get used to. Un-success is a lot more difficult to bear and the lessons to be learnt from these un-success(es) are many. I prefer to speak of success and un-success rather than success and failure (usual parlance). In an insidious way our brains might be wired for us to learn the variations of ball-speed and type of pitch as in baseball or the spin-wind effects on a golf ball, however well struck.

Success and un-success: the real-life example is Tiger Woods, how he fell from grace, un-successed, struggled and re-found his winning self and winning game. He went on to win his fifth Masters 2019 after failing for 14 years since his dominating runaway stretch of success of four Masters. He says, never give up, learn and re-learn but you must enjoy your game and be grateful for the blessing to be healthy to play competitively. Do not be seduced by the illusion of mastery.

XJWYKE: An airline booking code? No, it's your Cousins aka our magnificent 6 inspiring Grandchildren – Xuan, Jun yourself, Wen, Yin your

Quadrant IV: Illustration 5
Imagine SG vs. USA (Arctic Alaska)

sister, Kai and En who walked-ran at age 1 and communicates her moods and messages with her 'winking eyebrows'. Xuan at 12 gained the rare Brigadier Brooch national leadership award amongst all Singapore Girls' Brigades. Beginning with her love of the Bible, she incessantly read all the volumes of Harry Potter sequentially from beginning to end (unlike YY's symmetrical reading pairing of first and last ending into the middle.) At 3, Wen grew his first durian tree to a foot high but felt the gestation of 5 years was too long in Internet times and turned his attention as his primary class Internet advisor. The Alumnae of St Anthony's Girls School founded in 1879 (Motto: Via, Veritas, Vita – The Way, Truth & Life) selected Yin as the exemplar of young Anthonia! Kai at four, drew his first menu, offering his nouvelle patois cuisine in his own hand-writing font (research shows personal handwritten fonts influence choice and diner loyalty) for his make-believe hybrid-cuisine restaurant. And I have many more things to be proudly inspired by. En is a later arrival, in 2019. It pleased all of us, she's a natural educator enthused about learning and doing, as a 2-year old in play school acted like a self-appointed teacher's aide and calmed a fellow baby-mate by retrieving the pacifier. I took that as a blessing. (On the day and hour of her birth, I had on a day's prior notice enthusiastically agreed with Dr Lee Seng Tee to keynote the opening of the curated Exhibition of Diasporic SE Asia at Cambridge in honour of his 95th birthday. He had in the 1940s hoped to attend Cambridge instead of Wharton but for WWII and be a natural history specialist instead of banker.

To be sure, Xuan is your filial 'Eldest Sister-Cousin' or Tai-Ka Tze and Jun, you're Tai-Kor, 'Eldest Brother-Cousin'.

Grandparenthood – it's a higher calling of sorts. It's more of a conferment thrust upon you. You've to balance between a formal hierarchy of parental order of power and authority and being kicked upstairs as a Mentor Mother Superior with no power, no authority only mora-suasion. My sense after trial by error is that our Grandchildren by and large confer upon us the Grandparent-hood (not Mrs or Mr.) like an honorary degree or Honoris Causa, by 'high' example and achievement. So, my version is that you've to love your GrandOnes unconditionally, with no expectation of 'quid pro quo'. This brings to mind your younger Cousin Wen our elder Grandson who is quiet, thoughtful, understands systems and I spend quality time with him and his high achieving elder Sister Xuan.

They can call me anytime. Noah does.

Most of his relatives are reported by him to be 'asleep' or busy when he calls. He thought that highly unusual except this Grandfather, me. Well, he called me one early morning at 4.30a.m. to be exact, and I answered the call. Emergency? Robbery? No, he was just sleepless at Serangoon Gardens! After a short chat, yes it was pure sleeplessness. Yet school day starts soon for him as he has to be up at 6.00a.m. So, I persuaded him to make sure all the lights including bedside reading lights were switched off, and to say his prayers again with his eyes closed. And by happenstance, it worked, no problems, no complaints, just an innocuous happening.

One day Noah's Mother found his 'written note of the day' during his time in his kindergarten II. He hadn't shown it to anyone including Mother – 'My Grandfather loves me, this I know.' How sweet! He additionally then wanted me to be his 'Horse of choice' for the '2-3-generation Horse Race' but my Diamond-Anniversary lower back may not honour that with a

Quadrant IV: Enthusiasm, Faster & Forever 75

Quadrant IV: Illustrations 6-7
Black Swan Mirage ~ Lake Akali, Wyoming & Mighty Truck Drivers

sporting winning chance (so his Dad took that role and won). I do love him as I do all my Grand Friends – Grandma or NN says it best; she treats all fairly, more fairly the youngest one, Ms En.

Jun, as you may surmise, YY has befriended your Cousins, because in their innocence, they have a fine feel for authenticity, sincerity and simple good manners, a sense of goodness and fun, someone they can trust (no spilling to Mum or Dad, Scout's Honour!). As my dear late Professor UMKC Henry Bloch Business School Dean Dr TK Tan (PhD Cambridge) opined, "A good leader must first aspire to be a good man!" But trust is a good fugitive eluding oftentimes the best of all of us. Let me explain by sharing an incident. Four decades ago, my PA told me not to open my Executive Office door when I returned from an offsite meeting, as there's a chap sleeping on my couch. It was the late billionaire John Gokongwei, amongst the richest in all Philippines. When he awoke, I said that if I knew he was coming, I would have gotten him trusted praetorian security guards and a more suitable executive lounge to snooze in. Said he, 'I trust you-lah!'

Unthinkable? Maybe the new world of the quantum sponge accelerated learning of our Grandchildren's generation could narrow the gap between age, adulthood, brain development and maturation. Indeed, in earlier times Alexander the Great (with his great Mother Olympias) burst upon the scene at age 18 and conquered the known world by age 33, all the way from Greece to modern-day Afghanistan, Pakistan and India. Anecdotally, Mothers do play equally big roles as Olympias as in the cases of Henry Ford and General Douglas MacArthur. Both these personalities were the subject of study by my Freudian analyst-cum-specialist in the social psychology of leaders, Professor Abraham Zalesnik. who together with his Researcher Ann Desjardins, Zalesnik did an intriguing study some time ago in the mid-1960s. The General's Mother was so consumed with her son MacArthur that she took an apartment opposite West Point Academy to be the literary close alter ego to his evolving talents in life, study, peace and war.

Jun, years down the memory lane and when it's your time to marry, so the saying goes, you'll realise that all your parents' worrying about you begin to make more and more sense. (See more about this in paragraphs further down on the matriarchal Akela mums instead of the Ameri-Asian idea of Tiger Mums in Amy Chua's *Battle Hymn of the Tiger Mother*.)

Quadrant IV: Illustrations 8-9
Green Jigsaw: Corn, Ethanol & GM and Deforestation

Quadrant IV: Illustration 10
Akela-speak: Seeking Strategic High Ground

Heroes & Super Heroes: The joy of YY is that his Grandchildren think him their hero. In truth, I think you all are my ever superheroes! For you are the generation, together with Greta Thunberg (*Times* Person of the Year 2019) and others yet unknown to all. You have the highest order mission to save our little blue planet and our civilisation that we've been arguing about for the last 50 years. Climate change made 2018 the third hottest year since records were kept; climate change is also proven to have caused the first casualty of extinction – Australia's rat-like rodent, the Bramble Cay Melomys of the Torres Islands where the 'hobbit-like' first humans were also found.

Tao (Way) of Enthusiasm: If YY must mention any advice of sorts in one word, it's enthusiasm. Or more specifically the Tao (way) of enthusiasm, beyond just the enthusiasm of specific sport like running, skiing, skating, sailing, etc.

Invest in being unrelentingly enthusiastic. It changes the colour of your distinctive efforts and those of your colleagues. The Greek source of the

Quadrant IV: Illustrations 11-13
Eureka Ascent: YY Face to Face with Inner Child

word is *'entheos'*. Literally, 'en' in Greek is inside and 'theos' is god-like spirit. Metaphorically, it's akin to self like the gods! Everything that makes you different is self. Inside your*self* as Samurai Musahi says, too! So does my favourite Nobel Laureate Economist Robert Solow's endogenous factor (not exogenous or external) – the entrepreneurial spirit of innovation and change is from inside one's self.

We can have enthusiasm in many things. Enthusiasm for music, art, dance, fixing Lego or Gundam figurines, the list goes on. But if you think not of things but of a way of doing things, it's the Tao (way) of enthusiasm and developing the Enthusiasm-Edge Quotient or EnQ. This refers to the process and commitment; it manifests itself in grace and authenticity (no bluffing, no pretending). Besides the Greek origin, 'En' is also the Hanyu-Pinyin for grace and in Arabic it's 'Ridzuan' (Perak-Ridzuan is 'Abode of Grace'.) It's not for our personal glory or private agenda but for a mission – to be ever mission-minded and driven with enthusiasm which is visually impactful. The economics of the demonstration effect is easily more obvious than other important but more abstract ideas of leadership, invaluable though they are (complementary to the mix).

You must be internally strong to do it with poise and confidence! But if you would like, go speak to my YOG-NTU-2010 Games Village Troika with Uncle Andy Tan (now at NUH after serving Sports Singapore) and Uncle Selva (retired from National Institute of Education at NTU) as to what impressed them about YY. Together, our YOG Team had sustained enthusiasm over 18 months, in symphony practising the commitment late-in-life to the major-mission and (exemplary) 640-mini-missions adapted from the IOC. We had visualised multiple milestones with our NTU Team and YOG Team!

That when the YOG-Village started with the first meal with two Mayors Olympian Kunalan'68 and Minister Teo Ser Luck of the Games Village in attendance, and the dining marques ran out of bananas (not bottled water), who did they call?

You guessed right, YY! I made a couple of pressure-personal phone calls to the approved key suppliers and the crisis was solved. QED!

Unremitting enthusiasm of grace (no umbrage) that is continually nurtured can sustain you to wrestle persistent challenges that come your way, convince friends and enable a lead forward. VC Caroline McMillen

Quadrant IV: Illustrations 14-15
Traditional Transport Pre-StarTrek ('Beam me up!')

says of YY (and U were present) at the successful launch of *Univer-Cities Volume 3* on why she hosted UC2016 at Newcastle. She said it was the innocent telephone call-chat from Anthony Teo (your YY)! VC McMillen is an incredible witness; and her faculty colleagues beloved-ly call her the one with 'unrelenting charm'.

This tributary of enthusiasm spurred the Univer-Cities project to be sustained over four volumes during the course of a decade with the participation of senior international academic colleagues. The curated cover of Volume I 2013 was pantone black in serendipity (in retrospect) of the presumptuous Black Swan idea of univer-cities redefining the New Silk Road. The subsequent volumes were crimson Vol. II (in thanks to Alma Mater Fair Harvard), Cambridge Vol. III blue, and Singapore Vol. IV 2021 red and white.

I would be remiss if I overlook my mentor and dear pal Khoo Oon Theam whose focused enthusiasm of grace, fifty years ago, nudged his uncertain board members to buy the two-acre Stevens Road property for $500,000 which the downtown Palmer Road YMCA did not have. (He arranged to overcome every conceivable road block and even secured an in-principle bank borrowing in the meanwhile.) The property is now the multi-million dollar wildly successful Metropolitan YMCA. Khoo's enthusiasm of grace keeps him in youthful glow at 85!

Colour of Enthusiasm: First, the colour of success is enthusiasm! I have never forgotten that what got me my first job was my enthusiasm. As the Scotsman Personnel Director commented: it had meant a lot to him. The company-sponsored one-month executive Outward Bound School confirmed my colour of success – loads of enthusiasm. Then, the colour of enthusiasm that will define you or your intensity of interest or pursuit is not the usual White Swan, prim and pristine as they are. To restate with emphasis, the colour of enthusiasm is the exceptional Black (Swan) and its leading edge Crimson (Bill). My thinking was stirred by an encyclopaedic discussion with an Australian Swan Whisperer at Sunshine Coast by Pelican Waters with bevies of white swans and a rare couple of Mr & Mrs Black Swan.

If you want to be a winner, champion, entrepreneur, you must find your individual unique self and strengthen your inner entheos and strength.

Akela Mum's Total Learning of Qualities-Mix: To an often-heard complaint – there are so many qualities to master, about a dozen in all! Our beloved Cub-Scout Mistress also formally known as the alpha matriarchal leader Akela said, "That's what young Mowgli had to learn fast – the survival qualities-mix (and there are no shortcuts)." That mix of skills was essential in order for him to survive and thrive as a man-cub in his wolf-cub upbringing as part of the 'wolf-pack' (in the legendary Rudyard Kipling's *Jungle Book*). The man-eater tiger Shere Khan was on the prowl for Mowgli to keep the jungle free of humans. Total learning (every wolf a true dangerous-wolf) is akin to the idea of Total Defence in Singapore (until it's put to the test). But in the jungle, predatory death could strike suddenly.

Quadrant IV: Illustrations 16-18

Virtuality-Reality Matrix: Golden Minds-eye Back at Sherborne Rugger

That's why I am for the holism of Akela Mums; and not bi-polar ego-id centred Tiger Mums. It's the hard rock of knowledge drive, some skill-based and with an ever-present mother in practice and tuition (as in piano-forte?). Some children and mothers do succeed well, don't get me wrong. But it's not YY's way, the Tao of enthusiasm.

That's what Scouting taught me and I hold dear to this day. Sometimes with wavering faith I grow ever more convinced, that in our fast growing concrete (and green) jungles in SG and across the globe we all have to learn fast to survive well. As human beings with global human values we are filled with the milk of enthusiasm to win hearts and minds to lead, fight for our family, our home and our beloved Little Red Dot!

In modern academic language: the dilemma of facing complications and further complexities at the same time because they happen or exist simultaneously can now be expressed in the new idea of 'simultaneity'!

I eventually developed a Top Ten Action Note, but that's for another day.

Special Bonus of Finding Myself Hiking: Hiking over the 'pathos' of country-making (aka place-making) of SG, the island in the sun, has evoked the sentiment of what we call Home. For generations, we built friendships, families and enterprises, knew the land, we defended our land. My Dad served in civil defence pre-WWII; Eldest Brother Keng as a Colonel rising from a self-enlisted Private in the First Singapore Infantry Regiment; Sons and Nephews served National Service including OCS in Artillery, Commando and Sniper; and (thee our lead) amongst three Grandsons U, Wen and Kai in future will be replacing my three sons in NS. We have breathed the air, heat, hearth and dust of the earth, drank its aqua, owned pieces of the land, buried our forebears, relatives and friends and so wish to be returned to rest in SG earth that we are part of and learnt to co-own. *Majullah Singapura*. We're Singaporeans!

Eldest Brother Keng as a young lad during the war in the 1940s and for a few precious cents of wage, with artistic flair, prayer and ritual painted the ever-seeing spirit-radar 'double-eye' on the Singapore River tongkangs or river boats (built in boat-yards along the Kim Seng Road stretch of the River). The tongkangs transported lesser sacks of rice from the large steamships for discharge to the merchant godowns. The 'eyes' also invariably helped guide us all!

With Singapore's highest peak at only 520 feet, many are likely to feel Ulysses-ian, yearning to explore the world beyond. Yet there are hyperboreans, like anaesthesiologist Dr Chin Wui Kin who climbed Mt Everest in 2018 only to go missing in 2019 at 7,500-metres attempting avalanche-prone Mt Annapurna 'who' is usually beset with fickle

Quadrant IV: Illustrations 19-22
Inbox of Worldly Matters

weather. Another, is my fellow golfer Edmund Yong who at a young age precociously recommended his parents to send him for undergraduate studies in Queenstown, New Zealand, defined by picturesque alpine mountains, meadows and fjords. Edmund has not ceased climbing mountains (with a professional accounting, not climbing, certification of Chartered Accountant of England and Wales) including Mount Everest to the penultimate 5,650-metre Kala Patthar before the long final ascent. He saw the frozen marble-like bodies of the climbers of yore found along high Everest and he recently asked rhetorically why do they want to climb? Ask Nietzsche, ask the hyperboreans, and ask Mallory: "Because it's there." (Jun, share this letter with my pal Uncle Edmund Yong, your golfing Grand Uncle Yun's dear friend from NS days. It might intrigue him!)

As this is a long letter, Jun, I thought it merits highlights of four Black Swan appearances to show how the making of enthusiasm and its forever essence might make sense to you. The examples that follow are taken from your Dad and three of my primary experiences in early school days.

1. ***Black Swan-1: Process*** ~ 35 years ago your Dad, who won multiple Sports Colours at Sherborne, indelibly impressed upon me the timeless value of enduring 'forever enthusiasm' coincidentally through golf, again. He enthused the joys of the competitive spirit, as we shared quality time over Summer Saturdays' 36 holes (2x18-hole rounds) till the last North American daylight at about 9p.m. His moniker golf's true enthusiasm only prevails after striving to sink the last putt on the last hole! So it was in 2015 after 40 years of golfing, when that inspiration held true for YY and my enthusiasm resulted in golden success – the championship's gold at the 150th Anniversary Tanglin Club Golf Tourney. To be sure, that's what my long time 'golf kakis' (classmates Uncle Lock and Uncle Francis) say of their enjoyment golfing with YY even in the autumn of our lives!

2. ***Black Swan-2: Ephemeral Jackalope*** ~ 50 years ago on my epic 3,000-mile drive across America I met the elusive Scarlet Pimpernel-esque Jackalope weaving the narrative with imagination in the quiet early hours. Our minds are inclined to actualise the vision of twilight, mountains and trees of the final breath-taking drive up the Sierra Nevada via Yosemite onto to California with the grand old sequoia giant trees. It is just as 13th century Japanese Buddhist writer and poet suggests, "Enlightened vision is actualised in the mountains, grasses, trees, earth, stone, fences, and walls. Do not have any doubt about it." — Dōgen Eihei (1200-1253). Budding Vermont-Javanese Artist Himawan's creative medium of modernist textured illustrations in this book, viscerally weave you on a parallel 3,000-mile raven's flight of the blue BMW and black Mustang along Interstate 80. I tried and I found myself, hiking. I gather from anecdotal vignettes from my beloved Daughters-in-Law and more nuclearly, my Grandchildren. and your fellow alpha-matriarch Akela Mums (of Kipling's *Jungle Tales* and not Tiger Mums) 'who must be obeyed'. And in the pack council is the top Lone Wolf, the ever wise, original, and familial leader. While anticipating challenges to our young in their overtly greening concrete jungle of life, I must never be boring or write below their Plimsoll-line understanding.

1 ***Black Swan-3: Fount*** ~ 70 years ago upon my winning the Primary One Sports Day 25-yard Candle Race with a lightly toasted right palm (protector of the flame), that fount of Enthusiasm unsuspectingly popped up. It accelerated and multiplied. Eventually I parlayed

it evermore into tributaries: ubiquitously at NTU in the impossibly difficult creation in 9 months of the National Champion Draconika Chingay Parade Float 2009 and on to the making of the Herculean YOG 2010 Best IOC-approved Games Village in a record 15 months. My teams felt they had proud equity ownership and pleasingly remembered that these projects came to pass 'swimmingly' as though they were quite easily done, which was not the case. That, however, is the magic of Enthusiasm Forever to the day!

3. *Black Swan-4 Akela Mum* ~ 70 years ago and the ensuing five years, the Alpha Matriarchal Akela Scouting Cub Mistress appeared and taught me at an early age the total mix of the intrepidity of the true Wolf with the 'human-like 36-strategies'. These included team hunt-battles, guile, feints, lock-in chase and the last resort 36th strategy that entails the escape option – run for your life. Twice in YY's life, I had to choose this option to run away from my number one Ichiban who wanted me to be a tiger instead, with the lucky 'Faustus' bargain of loyal fealty in exchange for an 'allocated mountain' (no two tigers can co-exist on one mountain). It cannot happen as my Akela Mom(s) and I have sworn allegiance. I'm happy for that and am ever in praise of Akela Mums!

I hope being open and honest, limited by the words that I could muster, will reach you in heart, mind and spirit as it did with a 14-year old 'AdulTeen', then an up and coming young starlet Lisa Jakub. Lisa acted as the young daughter of the dispossessed father disguised as the housekeeper Mrs Doubtfire (acted by marque Hollywood star Robin Williams). Mrs Doubtfire on the set shared openly with her about his personal deep seated worries and demons as they co-starred in the classic film *Mrs Doubtfire* 25 years ago. Lisa recalls recently how much she appreciates Robin doing this and that it has had a good and lasting impact on her with an ensuing appreciation and friendship.

Quadrant IV: Illustrations 23-24
Howl of Pas-ture & Future: O Beloved Blue!

With true gratitude to my forebears and family, I thank my colleagues, friends, mentors, teachers, you and your Dad as fellow life-journey travellers for the grace of friendship in my 'Eureka Moment' aka 'Kodak Moment' – I FOUND MYSELF, HIKING!

For you, Jun, I hope you enjoy my sharing these personal thoughts with you and reading it in one go or in segments at your leisure. It's tough to pen a long letter, trying to maintain the flow without being boring, along a flexible structure. Thankfully the 'pathos of distance' helped hang it all together; and pray, may it be interesting and not too wild a ride (as for new words and meanings, Google is such a partner for timeous checking).

As your generation's life expectancy is to age 100 'may it be a joyous adventure' (as is in the Queen's Scout Certificate signed off by HM ER II). For YY, my actuarial expectation is living to 85 and eyeing the three Greek goddesses, who were sisters of Fate overseeing the thread of life and destiny: spinner Clotho, dispenser Lachesis and cutter Atropos.

Just in case the actuarial expectation is cut short, this letter is an extant and surviving peek into YY's little life, ever-striving in enthusiasm yet mindful to overcome the 'illusion of mastery'. Life and events are vicariously unpredictable.

Jun, be sceptical of the desk-bound scholar whose mastery of a given structure of knowledge can triumph in examinations but is questionable in the vagaries and tests of real life. Reflect critically of the Tiger Mum who drives along a similar path, whereas your alpha matriarch Akela Mum scans beyond knowledge, blending instinct, prescience into an amalgam of enthusiasm for the hunt like a mobile honing radar.

Trials and tribulations amidst oftentimes chaotic circumstances (as in pandemic times) are good case-studies offering the opportunity to learn to roll with the tough punches but to get up and take action. Recall how Chouhan led his fellow band of dispossessed and hiked-rode 1,250 miles to his wholesome home-village from the limbo of a COVID-19 lock-down in a primarily economic city, Bangalore.

Jun, YY asks of you to gird yourself with enthusiasm in breadth, depth and sinews for your own inner spirit to face the unknowns (some of which we don't/can't know or that we don't know yet).

So, I hope it isn't too wild a ride! 👣👣👣

Pray, Ulysses is my witness – to strive and not yield!

Ever,

The End (*What's Next?*). Selected globalists continuing the Univer-Cities Series. First is the University of Zurich's Dean of Evolutionary Medicine Professor Dr (Med) Frank Ruhli writing to his gifted young son Oskar on the unending evolution of the human condition post-COVID-19 and the Spanish Flu 1918.

For the following five postscripts and four attachments, please refer to Supplementary Quadrant VI.

Postscript One: *Curiosity* – I could not resist citing this word from *Alice in Wonderland* and the famous three words '*curiouser and curiouser*'. I first read them in the Radiant Readers Series of my 1951 Primary One Syllabus.

Postscript Two: *Jun* – This is not self-serving, but I kept the letters my Dad wrote me when I was away for two years in snowy Boston (and I squirrelled them away as a store of inspiration then and now.) My Mom was not given to writing, but I have had dear, dear conversations. How blessed we all have been: sisters, brothers, our sons and daughters and you our Beloved Grandchildren!

Postscript Three: *Giant Mentors* – My Scout Cub Mistress aka Akela who imparted the early full lessons of hunting and caring for the team-pack, my Scout Master who became the Chief Commissioner aka Black Bear, my devoted Rover Scout Master Henry Schooling aka Lone Wolf; and the scholar extraordinary young Law Dean Dr Tommy Koh who so kindly advised me on 'what Harvard means to alumna/us' (now known as *The Crimson Essays*) and launched me on my published writings.

Postscript Four: *The Future's Arriving* – New Zealand has just made River Whanganui a Legal Person just as Toledo Ohio (my first stop after 600 miles straight from New York City) has made Lake Erie a Legal Person. Artificial Intelligence or AI next?

Postscript Five: *Warning 2019* – Where have all the birds gone?

ATTACHMENTS

Attachment I – *Emailed Letters from HBS Professor Warren McFarlan* on my provost-ship of HBS Global Forum on "The PRC & Post-WTO" in Shanghai 2004. 'From Sentosa AMP'81 to Shanghai'04, we both rose to the challenge'; and the 25th Anniversary of embedding social enterprise in the MBA Programme at HBS 2019. Few amongst the invited guests have engaged as long as you in the past 25 years.

Attachment II – $100 million inherited assets in return for estimated 1.5-year $30 million of incremental sweat and guile; posted by my NTU-YOG Village hands-on Deputy Andy Tan, 15 January 2011.

Attachment III – Testimonium 2017 on how NTU became Top 11th Globally.

Attachment IV – Ode to Primary One teacher Mrs Chelvan: 'Reading maketh a full man'.

Quadrant V
Warp Speed, Fastest & to the Future

Designed in a circular wheel for re-entry to engage at any preferred choice of where you start to read, this segment addresses the issues of warp speed & constancy of the true U as noted in the opening paragraph of the Letter. Identified as Quadrant V, it serves to not disrupt the trend of thought and flow of the Letter in the earlier four Quadrants. Essentially, it follows through on the impact of warp speed *to* 'Why, this quilt of many distances and places?'

Allow me to reiterate the circular context of the **5,000-word five Quadrants**, as follows

> LETTER TO GRANDSON JUN, **QUADRANT I**: HIKING, FAST & IN FEAR
>
> LETTER TO GRANDSON JUN, **QUADRANT II**: DRIVING, FASTER & FARTHER
>
> LETTER TO GRANDSON JUN, **QUADRANT III**: WHY FASTER & HIGHER?
>
> LETTER TO GRANDSON JUN, **QUADRANT IV**: ENTHUSIASM, FASTER & FOREVER
>
> LETTER TO GRANDSON JUN, **QUADRANT V**: WARP SPEED, FASTEST & TO THE FUTURE

Jun, what is warp speed when applied to your interest in golfing through the looking glass eyeing Tiger Woods' ups & downs? Golfing great Tiger Woods took 21 years to win 82 PGA Titles. The first 41 took 7 years whilst the second half took 14 years. For busy observers it felt like time flew fast past. Maybe not for Tiger as he suffered a dogged struggle sprinkled with lack of enthusiasm. If we look at it in a compressed space-time or an equivalent of our pal pooch or canine life-years, it's the equivalent of 'two canine years' to win his redeeming 15th Major (but the first 41 were done in one). Overall, his all-time 82 wins at warp speed of the first 41 were achieved in one canine year with the fearsome 'Tiger Roar'.

His second 41 took two canine years of quieter internal struggles of a 'weary mind' but sustained by his life's enthusiasm for the philosophy, tradition of the game, re-building the will to win and matching his first 40 wins with a wondrous feat of winning a decisive 5th Masters' Title. Tiger eminently portrays the moments of mastery after all the practising in trying to achieve the elusive absolutist nirvana of compleat mastering. So in real life, the reality is that you've to cope, learn, strive and not yield from failed attempts or un-success. Training and practice with purpose are recorded into the 'to win suspense account' till you win.

Remember, Jun, process is a tested way of learning and moments of mastery are more akin to a cataclysmic Little Red Dot when everything coalesces to a climactic outcome. It doesn't describe the struggles involved. That's where sustained enthusiasm is so crucial. Your winning the Primary Inter-School Floor Ball Championship in that two-year window was that Moment of Mastery when, in your aura of leadership, you marshalled your Team.

McIlroy points to the added enthusiasm edge of Tiger who "Thinks and dreams of things that other people don't think are possible."

Jun, let's not be blindsided by the desk-bound scholar's take of mastery (of knowledge mainly and some skills). When you think and dream of feeding tributaries of enthusiasm then the illusion of mastery becomes clearer.

As an aside at this juncture where Tiger searched for his winning ways, YY's so glad that you gave your all at your first week-long US Kids World of Golf Championship 2019 at The Plantation course located in the southern Malaysian Peninsula. You competed with the best of your age group without fear. Yet your initial un-success gave you more takeaways to learn and improve your game. The competition battle scars emboldened you for the next many foray games around the region. You bounced back at the pre-Christmas 2019 Phua Thin Kiay Junior Invitational on a co-winner score but ending with a runner-up position on countback as your putt hovered at the edge of the cup with a bogey 'par for the game of golf' (respect that fine line). Oh dear! Next tournament.

The warp speed upturn of Tiger's latter period to winning his 5th Masters in 2019 is like a tiger crouching as an uprising phoenix-dragon. His Mum

Quadrant V: Illustration 1

Re-conquering Resurrecting Transfear

like your Dear Mum is an Akela Mum who nudged you and him to greater heights, bounding back repeatedly.

There are other hungry rivals eager to capture Tiger's place of most serial wins next only to Jack Nicklaus. The new generation of winners like Rory McIlroy, Jordan Spieth and Justin Thomas signal infinitely tougher competition to come.

That's why Tiger's 5th Masters is even more startlingly awesome and shokku as in Japanese.

He overcame the classic new 'trans-fear' or simply transfear, Octopus of Fear. This is in the confusing land of fear when Tiger doubted many would trust him after all his personal troubles and auto accidents. He didn't even trust his own existing swing! When fear re-emerges in your mind, everything turns upside down. Right swing becomes suspect swing. False is true. Lies become truth. It gets complicated in that fears and phobias might evolve into new ones living in the discontinuous gaps that new combination(s) of disciplines may have to be called on to help solve. Additionally, at your individual level you have to find (or have already found) your true self which is what makes a difference in these between spaces (that are inter-spatial). Only you with your own values and vision can see the way ahead especially where moral and other choices need to be made.

You imagine what your situation might be if you were Snow White and the Seven Dwarfs turned into the force of evil like Anakin Skywalker in *Star Wars* transforming into the evil Darth Vader. Then the seven would be the Seven 'Devil' Dwarfs with their terrible opposite qualities (new-original combo) – Leader's Charlatan-Doc with Hyper-Dopey, Easygoing-Grumpy, Wretched-Happy, Sleepless-Sleepy, Boastful-Bashful and SilentSpreaderCorona-Sneezy. Covid battle over? Here come the covid variants!

The world can be cruel. But the Jackalope seems ever free, audacious, bold in its temerity of spirit yet 'invisible'. The very idea is puzzling but it has intrigued my optimist senses ever since I 'met' the human-like eccentric March Hare (1865) of Lewis Carroll in Radiant Readers during first grade at school.

Soon, innocently I was reading the darker tensions of good and evil in *Snow White (1812) and the Seven Dwarfs*. There were also the German Brothers Grimm's Fairy Tales (Tale Number 53) with the maleficent Queen and her every present-day's concern as to who's the fairest of all (in contrast to Carroll's less noted wise White Queen who encouraged Alice to think about the exciting future).

From a trans-disciplinary way in golf you've the benefit of learning from specific golf psychology and generic sports psychology (of successful teams like the All Blacks of NZ with a remarkable 75:25 win-loss record in the past hundred years). The in-between space might have to be dealt with by the seemingly unrelated new and different disciplines, for example, of contemplative Zen as applied in the art of the Samurai (individual like a lone golfer). It's best practised by Musashi, the all-time survivor of some 67 sword duels. Likewise in this day and age, there is the reformed offender John Crilly who sprang into action during a terrorism attack on the London Bridge 2019 using a humble fire-extinguisher to fearlessly cow a two-knife armed killer who had stabbed two to death; saying after that he was "prepared to die" to save others.

In short, when you find the gap in transfear, you have to get rid of it before it accumulates, or mutates to populate the gap! In essence, the two principles of dealing with transfear are firstly, to expel this alien when found and if not possible at one go, like good housekeeping cleanse and bridge the gap whenever it opens.

Fast forward, serendipitously useful in the pandemic times of 2020 and 2021, be socially responsible.

In social distancing (that gives additional meaning to Nietzsche's *Pathology of Distance*) we must cleanse the gap in transfear! There is the pathology of COVID-19 transmission through walk by contact via silent spreaders including yourself who may be one. There is the circuit-breaker or lockdown when home distance learning becomes boring. And there is the worrying about friends and everything. Remember clean your hands, clean the door knobs, wear a mask and … cleanse the gap in transfear!

Warp Speed Rhythm in Logistics: Logistics is as old as horse-drawn supply wagons. Today it's the veritable all-season durable trucker who crisscrosses the big country 24/7. We met such men (and now more women) at the truck-stop diners along the interstate highways as we drove from New York to California. We spoke half in jest about the greasy eggs and caffeine shots of coffee that looked like dish water. In truth these are our hardy heroes, with a nonchalant selflessness who serve our every need right down to the re-rated lowly toilet rolls – recently the subject of squirrel-like 'common' panic buying during the COVID shutdowns. But the enormity of the truth when the COVID pandemic struck is that folks were seen queuing at the malls, wholesale outlets, Walmarts, Costco, et al. Likewise medical and support staff at the hospitals needed to don survival kits such as simple masks and safety-wear to provide medicines and ventilators for the ICUs to save the afflicted.

To the truckers, the diner stops are their respite, the social network of pals, news, helicopter traffic cops, unpublished road closures, hand-over continuity and the unstated bravado. A Bond of Brotherhood (that only truckers imbibe in full measure) exists across the land when the truckers sustain prolonged absence from home and loved ones. It was lovely to behold as they 'accepted' our intrusion at the many diner stops, as always with their understated calm in the face of a truly physical pathology of long distances cum survival alertness. They know a good steed (and a fellow cowboy) when they see one ridden by our dear tall Yankee graduate doctor Frank in his acquired mid-west swagger alighting from his matt-black Mustang Cobra. In their fondest imagination of racing Ford's Lee Iacocca-Baby, they inspect the Mustang in the carpark lot and banter with Frank as we walk to a 'lucky' available table led by a cheery local lass 'hostess'. What came next was a little surreal (an out of body view of the scene) like a slow-motion tension of the unexpected, unexpectedly geniality versus hostility to an intrusion of a couple of city-slickers, one could recall the stories in the sixties of trucker-commuter highway mix-ups. In truth, it was closer to a later Steven Spielberg's movie about a psychiatric anthropology of a highway *Duel* of a trucker and a California commuter. But, today and in retrospect, my heart strings strum the camaraderie of *The Brotherhood of Broadway* plus the unanticipated gems found 'On The Road' created by CBS Charles Kuralt every Sunday running for an amazing 50 years.

In pensive times, the memory flashes before me. I now understand this ever-resilient all-weather marathon-performance of truckers' receptiveness to Frank, Soong and me.

It's *The Brotherhood of Broadway* (wide-freeways). We're the younger 'brotherly' co-riders for the 2,000 miles on Freeway-80 from Michigan to California. We've followed their rhythm, passed, rested, caught up with some, but not all, along that week in June! The truckers were on their ultimate personal icons with aero-dynamic hoods befitting the board skills of their DASH (dedication, achievement, sensibility & highway-horsemanship). Their acumen recalls the best of Sioux horse whisperers who guide their man and mustang as one ('sunkawakan' in Sioux Lakota). Compare their 500-horse powered Kenworth Truckers Truck to our combo of two timeless classic sport-cars, a Mustang-Cobra and racer BMW2002!

We kept a respectful pace at permitted high speeds representing a resonance of the rising young drivers of America who took every challenge that the highway gave, just as the veteran truckers did.

Fast forward to 2020 – Wyoming owner-trucker Darrell Woolsey zooming towards Rock Springs (our rest stop at El Rancho 50-years ago on the Interstate-80). He's the now 52-year old YouTube streaming blogger, self-quarantined in his 'one-man-operated' truck yet happy with his built-in bed and breakfast studio 'compartment-tel'. He's on the road, with loads paying sometimes $2 per mile at best. His networks of delivery assignments is through his friend-dispatcher located in neighbouring

Quadrant V: Illustration 2
Socio-Anthropological Truckers: Brotherhood of the Hi-Way

Iowa's Cedar Falls. He is heading towards home, hopefully soon, to his family (wife and three high-school children) – like so, as with 3 million truckers in America. See Woolsey's story "Alone on the Road" at <https://truckerworld.uk/2020/03/alone-on-the-road-a-truckers-long>.

Little wonder, at the friendlier trucker stops, owner-truckers could relate to the cool 'racer-driver' Soong in his BMW. The majority of truckers, like Darrell Woolsey, own a similar German Daimler 2016 Freightliner truck. It is a reliable power-engineered all-weather road-holding distance runner that can easily do 50,000 miles annually or 16 times across America.

Additionally, in the land of the free and home of the brave, owner-operators who went to the 'university of hard knocks' (Soong and I from a well-known east-coast business school) benefited royally again, poignantly in the 2020 pandemic (costing about the price of a fully-costed Mercedes 250 after taxes in Singapore). To think about it, with all warp speed of the technology of logistics and fulfilment of the orders of enormous giants such as Amazon, Costco and the like, delivery still comes down to the hybrid high-speed massive 9-ton physical truck and the last mile(s) on the interstate network.

Empathy with hikers & truckers 2020: Like trucker Darrell Woolsey in self-imposed quarantine as he drives his truck for deliveries interstate across the USA, there is migrant worker Rajesh Chouhan in COVID lockdown in India 2020. I can feel the gritty enthusiasm moving this young married migrant worker to the do-able but improbable low budget 'hike-hitchhike combo' idea to reach home 1,250 miles north of Bangalore in ten days versus being stranded, jobless and languishing in locked-down limbo. He courageously touched the agonising guts of ten fellow villagers and convinced them to join this walkathon, rising to a true marathon! Their point-of-no-return first critical mini-mission happened swiftly, emboldening them. The successful breakout of the Bangalore police cordon and the rest are now (legendary) history. Their journey was a mix of intensity hiking at 5mph in blistered and bloody feet (by comparison, my 3mph over 30 miles was a cake walk) and at times a rapidly faster 70mph hitch-hike along India's interstate. They hitched rides from truckers on distinctly gaudy Indo-UK Ashok-Leylands and Indo-German Bharat-Daimler Benz 'Indo-fatherly' (rather than 'American brotherly') travelling from Bangalore north to his beloved family village near the border with Nepal. Chouhan's story was reported on CNN on 31 May 2020.

Question Zero for You Jun: Do you need to choose between academic studies and golf? You may not need to. Let me explain. Your young Auntie Dr (Med) Katie MD was cited with praise by her UCLA Children's Hospital Dean for Paediatrics at the 2020 graduation for her enthusiastic thought & practice leadership and patient-care displayed during her required three-year internship. We were part of Katie's teenage years as GrandMa is her God-Mother (and of interest is one thread of this energy bunny, you are, too). Katie noted her high school twin-track participation in maths & sciences with golfing (and also as a qualified soccer referee). So between the twin-tracks you may not necessarily need to limit yourself to either studies or golfing. Katie combined the two and found the space in between – Paediatrics? She resolved the dilemma in shaping the in-between disciplinary space by the pursuit of optimising 'paediatrics for ever-healthy youthfulness' a necessary foundation for healthy longevity with the mix of maths-science and golf-soccer!

Katie thereafter won an appointment at Seattle's Virginia Mason Paediatric Medical Center near her childhood home to serve her city community that had nurtured her. The surprising bonus was that her new boss, to her amazed delight, was her physician in her pre-teen years. It was like a magic circle of 'hard hard work' that took her across the American continent (beyond the usual regionality) from pre-Med at Seattle's UW in the West, Med-School at SUNY in the East, and back to the West at a post-Med UCLA internship to home again!

Warp Speed Valuations in Uncertainty: As 2019 sprinted its course deep into December All-American Baseball Legend Babe Ruth, from beyond, jolts baseball's eternal field of dreams through his fear-striking baseball bat which auctioned for a cool US$1 million. In uncertain times, you might note that art and 'good old times' memorabilia skyrocket in value ranging from baseball cards, championship rings, jerseys to bats (versus the average bat price to that of players, ranging from US$50 to 20,000 times). If Frank had kept his Mustang in mint condition, it would now be worth $500,000.

The Mud Hens' long-time field of dreams is part of the social capital and connectedness quilt of the Toledo-ean community celebrating their favourite son Tom Matchick who was part of the Detroit Tigers World Series Championship Team 1968. Their culminating moment of mastery "We don't know when" but in 1968, it was baseball's greatest comeback from 0-3 to winning 4-3. It highlights baseball's beauty, grace and humility of Superhero Champion slugger Al Kaline (who passed away in 2020 at 85, forever a hero-in-my-heart). Another unusual talent of The Team 1968 enjoying the flexy feature those days of the versatile all-round fill-in player (called the Utility Infielder, fielding to pitching and batting in the pitcher-in-the-line-up) was Toledo-ean Tom Matchick (No.2 Tigers' Uniform).

Americans colour their world of sports and entertainment personalities with grandiose accolades and serious greenbacks or real money. In 2019, the baseball Super-Heroes New England's Boston Red Sox after 120 years is worth some US$3.2 billion (or 8 times the transacted price-tag 17 years ago of about US$400 million).

Warp Speed Superheroes Unleashed: Americans love their superheroes from Batman, Mutant X-Man to Joker and The Jedi to good young potential Jedi Anakin Skywalker who joined the dark force and became the dastardly Darth Vader. Hollywood transforms these comic characters live through *Imagineering*. This is achieved via astute directing and cinematographic alchemy. As a mark of success they transform the characters into unrestrained make-believe reality blockbuster movies and pure capitalist money box-office revenues (not profits) like venture capital practices of the early 2000s. When the warp speed is slowed to a contemporary pace, there is a reflection of some of the tensions in American society between the light and the dark sides. In war, there are the warrior Minutemen of 1776 fighting for America's freedom to the many wars thereafter like in Afghanistan, Iraq and Vietnam unfortunately with occurrence of atrocities like the 1968 My Lai Massacre of innocents. In public life there's the respected patrician global-centric 41st President George Herbert Walker Bush, three centrists in Bill Clinton, George W. Bush and Barack Obama and then the unorthodox U.S.-centric 45th President Donald Trump (whom some unkindly dismiss as 'pusillanimous' or Latin for small soul). Will the real USA please stand up? May my letter bring some added light to your budding global view and understanding of America as a living work in progress, besides Professor Jill Lepore's well-argued historic analysis.

In America's make-believe world of the performing arts, there is the ultimate pinnacle of recognition, the Oscar. It was established by its own Academy of Motion Pictures Arts & Sciences with about 7,500 peers of directors, actors, cinematographers and other professionals of note. Your YY knows this as he has been in a film venture with his HBS classmate David Hamilton and then fiancée (now spouse) Deepa Mehta whose third movie *Water* (Trilogy of *Fire, Earth* & *Water*) won a Best Foreign Movie Oscar Nomination 2005 with Mexico's *Labyrinth* and Germany's *Other People's Lives* (about the dreaded East German intelligence agency, the Stasi) which pipped the other two on votes and won Oscar 2005. It was well funded over the other two low-budget movies. So near yet so far. Despite the ecstasy and the taste of lost star-dust, it launched the movie career of Hamilton & Mehta with the epic movie based on Salman Rushdie's *Midnight's Children,* the sagacious making of India and Pakistan at the stroke of midnight on 15 August 1947. The story was told through the intertwining lives of six Indo-Pakistanis and adapted for the screen by Rushdie himself through the power of Deepa's personal persuasive conversation in

New York! David and I wondered in our musings the origins of this power; and I relate to him the medieval abbotess, counsellor and alchemist Hildegard of Bingen (1098-1179). She was the early pioneer of gender equality, who with women folk won the right to manufacture ale to a specified quantity and quality. She was known for her many volumes of medicinal writings and cures, and had held in trust Crusaders' co-created wealth as they fought in Jerusalem. She benefacted convents, schools, universities and hospitals (fast forward to these days, rather like Melinda Gates-French in America and on our island, Ms Gek Khim and Ms Margaret Lien).

Then one day David and I went to the Seattle Safeco Field to watch the Boston Red Sox play the hometown Seattle Mariners with the home-run hitting Ken Griffiths Jr and the sure all-round hitter Suzuki Ichiro. David turned to me, in the midst of the game, saying "How come you know so much about baseball all the way back to our Boston days in the late sixties with the Detroit Tigers, Minnesota Cardinals. Any real usefulness?" Ah yes, not only is it Americana's field of dreams, but on the road near Iowa's North Platte truck stop when a trucker's banter with Frank (and his Mustang-Cobra) found that he started this drive from Michigan, it got everyone talking of the Detroit Tigers. Conversation got into the thick of the Championship World Series'68 recounting Al Kaline turning a one-run deficit with a hit-single scoring two runs and the resultant go-ahead-winning-run in Game 5 against the St. Louis Cardinals (overall: clawing up to 2-3 with 2 games to go). Then the legendary 0.450 (hitting 45 of 100 at bat) assassin Pinch Hitter (a switch inserting a reliable hitter to 'pinch' a survival hit) Gates Brown, a reformed streetwise kid who served time in prison, smashed the winning hit-double pushing in a run to get the Tigers into the World Series in the first place! Both were beloved Tigers who played their entire baseball career with Detroit. Imperceptibly, I could sense an added socialisation momentum into a fungible Brotherhood of Broadway!

Oscar Award: An Oscar is the priceless paradigm of acclamation by your peers embodied in the 'art deco' stylised Oscar Statue of the indomitable knight in golden sheen with a golden 'Crusader' sword. Even eastern socialist Zhang Yimou, John Woo, Ang Lee and maverick Korean Bong of the *Parasite* shocking unequal reality in Korea and others partake of this capitalist model.

Quadrant V: Illustration 3-4
Jackalope: Ever-present or Shape-changing?

The Oscar aside, the global cinematic-magic lingua tells the tales of the one man of steel, Superman, flying at the speed of a bullet in comics, on the silver-screen and in tattoos! Young folks brilliant as they are, some truly aspire to be Superman. But, Jun, I am glad you are more worldly anchored.

Quo Vadis Jackalope: A Jackalope is as real as it is to me even without this cinematographic magic medium that was brought to the global silver screen in movies such as Madagascar, Rio, Lion King, Frozen and Hybrid Avatar.

Beyond the hybrid zonkey comes this unbelievable Jackalope in fine artististic sketches that may be manifest in cloning or crossbreeding as time goes on. Be that as it may, the imagination of the Jackalope (to be more precise, the Western Jackalope of the hills in the cowboy state of Wyoming) still runs wild.

I reminisce about the high hills where the Mississippi keeps running (via its tributary Missouri-North Platte River into Wyoming). In 2019, in the lowlands with the mountains in the background, you my Dear Grandson Jun were at your first US Kids World Golfing Championship in the southern Malaysian peninsula. I share my reminiscing of the past half century of lessons and the emergent two-way inspirations for sharing. It comes back to the Jackalope, as though it was as surreal as in the TV Serial 'X-Files' with Gillian Anderson; and me saying aloud, "The Truth lies out there, is it true, the Jackalope?"

The mountains echoed, "The Truth lies out there, is it true, the Jackalope?" Or was it the cowboy folklore of the Jackalope's miming human voice to a perfect pitch?

I thought I heard a faint refrain, "R U an educated-man or a Jackalope like me born to keep running as the Mississippi does ..."

Ever the reality test: 'R U AN EDUCATED-MAN?' In short, it is Jackalope's RUAE.

... Is it Educated Enthusiasm?

Footnote 1: Unsighted Licence in various tongues (in cheek!) reportedly issued to the curious many believed to be like so -

Jackalope Hunting Licence

Verily permits annual hunting of the said specie (one only), caught alive tenable between midnight and the 1st on only 31st day of June under the Fishing & Wildlife Rules, yet unpassed.

Chamber of Commerce

Douglas, Wyoming

Footnote 2: *Why Jackalope?* Like an octopus of time, it's latched on my long-term memory of the 3,000-mile drive across America.

What feeds this octopus of time? Is it humans' enchantment, fantasy, fear and lure of the unknown celebrated in the genre of Melville's *Moby Dick* and the white whale, Hemingway's *The Old Man and the Sea* and the giant marlin, *Twenty Thousand Leagues under the Sea* and the fear tingling carnivorous giant octopus, King Kong, Godzilla, Jurassic Park and the ferocious T-Rex and the unending quest for the Loch Ness Monster?

Finally: Why, why? Perhaps, woman and man must invent ideas and be able to visualise to see one's self on a hike, a drive or even in a grain of sand as William Blake would have it, alas:

> *To see a world in a grain of sand*
>
> *And a heaven in a wild flower,*
>
> *Hold infinity in the palm of your hand*
>
> *And eternity in an hour.*

Pandemic and Variants have been ruthless, virulent and indiscriminate infections to afflict death with stealth and suddence. They shut down villages, cities, countries and societies to the ends of the world except the "Noah's Arks" of remote islands and furthest Arctic Canadian Territory of Nunavut. Jun, all this is happening along with your generation inheriting the most inventive 100-year of human life through the accumulative 2000-year AD – Anno Domini since the time of Jesus Christ.

2020 shall be the Year Zero of Anno Corona:

Despite all our science, research and the constant strategic scanning of the environment, the COVID virus slipped through at warp speed across the globe and whacked the human race like no other calamity ever, probably since the Great Plague of the Middle Ages in Europe of 1350AD decimating a population of some 500 million to about 300. Though current fatalities are not in those magnitudes, the more virulent variants of the second wave have spread at warp speed all the way up Mount Everest!

Humankind is besotted to predictability of our valued human-life. Health and happiness are mutually encouraged by the increasing longer life-spans or longevity. Your generation as a new norm would hit 100!

Everyone knows that the two certainties of life are death and taxes (with a higher focus on taxes). The COVID-19 virus has a scary focus on early and unexpected death and vigilance against the virulent variants.

Always remember that nothing is truer than U – Yes, 'YOU'.

At the end it wasn't the crow that charted the shortest distance of a journey but the Raven. It was the Raven that flew back to Noah in his

Ark with a twig, the sign that the Great Flood had subsided! Noah knew himself, he listened, he read the signs, 'engineered' the Ark to hold the flora, fauna and family in the continuity of humankind. Remember Noah – he's a natural process genius, though with some higher assistance!

Does Trump know himself? First, he's got to understand what is truth? (Literal Latin: Quid est veritas?) He is noted for having issued over 15,000 'alternative facts' (like lies) and at a rate of five to ten words each, could amount to 75,000-150,000 words or three to seven times the length of this 25,000-word letter.

In the poesy of sweet natural justice in Hilaire Belloc's light verse, Mathilda suffered the fate for life-long disregard of her aunt's strict regard for the truth and was consumed in her house fire when the London Fire Brigade ignored her final and truthful urgent summons. (Trump burnt his bridges to the truth and eventually lost his re-election for a second term.)

For completeness in view of the virulence of a pandemic with exponential infection like a widening areal summer forest fire, we may ask was there enough surveillance of such pestilence. The answer seems to be a 'Yes, the 43rd President Bush recognised it in a 2005 presidential address' and followed up by enacting laws for the emergency stockpile, infrastructure and processes in the omnipresence of the now famous Dr Fauci then and now with his 2017 follow-on formal pandemic warning to the 45th President Trump.

It wasn't systemic failure. It points to Barbara Tuchman's characterisation of the human beings' *March of Folly* tracing from the fall of Troy in the Greek-Trojan War to the American-Vietnam War, ignoring the mosaic of evidence at those material times (presently including the chosen one who dismantled the key unit for fighting pandemics). At Troy it was the leader who ordered the artisan to hack-off the lintel atop the main gate of Troy (in order to permit the head of the Greek wooden horse with Greek warriors hidden inside) which exposed an engraved warning, 'Whosoever removes this is responsible for the death of Troy'.

Do the presidents of PRC, Korea and Singapore know themselves? History would say yes; and doing what's right, saving lives, caring for their people's livelihoods and preparing for recovery in the new normal with needed social distancing. Jun, you know as you're the Social Distancing Ambassador for your class!

Quadrant V: Illustration 5

*Jackalopean Armature: Embedded in Psyche,
Emboldened my Enthusiasm*

To restate, perhaps, if everyone is deeply enthusiastic for their fellow beings' well-being, and are more self-aware, authentic (no bluffing) and disciplined to be socially responsible as in total defence, it might approximate the tough but happier and benign China, Korea and Singapore profile-experience; rather than the unhappier Brazil and India.

Thankfully, our modern-day heroic hiker cum barefoot hitch-hiker Chouhan found himself, tested, tougher and safer at home and hearth rather than jobless and in limbo in faraway Bangalore, 1,250 miles south of his home. Still struggling in his home village, yes but with more abundant healing love.

Jun, in this 25,000-word conversation via this letter to you, my Dear Eldest Grandson (aka, Honourable Tua Soon in Fukien) I celebrate finding myself, hiking.

YY's tales of 5 to 30 miles seem a cake-walk compared to Chouhan till you add in the 3,000 trek-drive across America to firstly finding myself, refreshed in the fullness of the pathology of distance and enthusiasm. Secondly, like Dr Emmett Brown in the 1985 blockbuster movie Back to the Future, I've always dreamed of seeing the future and particularly of this behemoth, America. It was a vista-vision glimpse in time, space and apparent interstices. It did scare me some, but reflectingly evoked in me an abiding feel of this unfinished experiment that is the 'United States of America' with its show-and-tell and incredulous work-in-progress unfolding often generating angst (for example, in the Trump years) and soothed with the allied promise of its continuing possibilities. In the intervening years it enabled me to collaborate and compete with my fellow American colleagues, rivals and business competitors.

YY's in Seventh Heaven, I did it with the beat of an enthusiastic heart. The enchantment of the unbeknownst emboldened my enthusiasm. Who would be so foolhardy to create the pure greenfield Chingay Float'09 and the massive-mission NTU-YOG Village 2010 via adaptation and re-jigging IOC's 640 strategic mini-missions. I did and successfully!

Truth be told, it was intuitively easier versus dealing with 3,500 miles of twists, turns, driving 'mile-highs' and meeting every challenge that the roads, weather and traffic threw at us!

Once is not enough?

Presently even with the latest top of the line dream BMW 740Li super sport saloon?

YY will opt out for a myriad of prime reasons – not perfect serenity. Just old age. Bucket list?

Ain't even a worthy last wish!

Mate, it gets better yet. There will be a 'Recce nuevo Jackalope-australis' at Jackalope Hotel by the Mornington Peninsular, a scenic drive by the Tasman Sea from Melbourne!

5 April 2020, Year Zero AC

Year 1 AC: COVID strikes back at India in warp speed on serial waves and variants, infecting about half a million a day. Deadly comparison: YOG at Singapore 2010's 'no bananas' pales to COVID in India 2021's 'no oxygen'!

Quadrant VI
Sweet Conclusion

Dear Jun,

Jun, when you've 15 minutes to yourself, you might want to dive in here. YY once made a mistake by asking his World Fellowship's referred VIP Guest-in-SG what he would be pleased to do after our breakfast till lunch's end.

'Monsieur Teo, you don't know that I never had 15 minutes to myself to just do anything I want,' replied the former three-term PM of Canada, Jean Chrétien.

So he was intrigued to go on a 'one square kilometre' visit of cosmopolitan religious worship ranging from the 1835 Armenian Church to Masjid Al-Burhan, St Joseph's Portuguese Mission, Kuan Yin Temple, Sri Krishnan Temple & Maghain Aboth.

Why?

Because, contrary to our economic prowess, we're not Philistines! He let forth a huge guffaw; and we had a convivial nouvelle cuisine lunch atop 70-storey Westin Tower, with petit 'beaver's tail' crepe dessert à la Rideau Canal by Westin Ottawa.

May you enjoy your visit to this Quadrant VI – Sweet Conclusion!

This is like dessert to end a 6-course dinner after the five phases of apertif, hors d'oeuvres, le plat principal, salade and plateau de fromages in this 25,000-word letter.

One day, Jun we'll go to the Jackalope Hotel at Mornington by Melbourne to their Doot Doot Doot experience and savour their sweet conclusions!

These short notes complement the letter. They provide sweet endings to bring a richer contextual feel and depth of lasting taste to matters I have described in a conversational manner of speaking and letter-writing.

Specifically, I have done this so as not to complicate the letter and disrupt its continuity, flow and rhythm.

As you can see, the matters are as follows:

Postscript One: *Curiosity* and *Mrs Chelvan's 4-Code* – I could not resist citing this word (from *Alice in Wonderland's* famous three words 'curiouser and curiouser' of the Radiant Readers Series). My Primary 1 teacher Mrs Chelvan opened my mind to the timeless 3Rs – Reading, 'Riting & 'Rithmetic. Now even Harvard Business School thinks curiosity is a novel quality to have in yourself and in the life of corporations it can be a business competitive edge.

Through first Radiant Reader, Mrs Chelvan's 4-Code imbued in me:

a. *Code 1 ~ Fidelity* to your friends and mission, as in the fifty-year devotion to my Alma Mater Harvard and in remembering society in social enterprise (Letters from Professor Warren McFarlan).

b. *Code 2 ~ 'Rithmetic*: Always do your sums as reflected in inheriting $100 million assets in reality in exchange for investing the sweat of our brows in the YOG 2010 Village at NTU.

c. *Code 3 ~ Be a Sport:* Take Part in Primary School's Lighted Candle Race (me, YY) resisting the wind, remember Horatio Nelson's wind-assisted two-line of battleships in an unorthodox geometric side-winder attack; and in karate-kicking off the Floor Ball to win the championship (you, Jun). In Nelson's case, he realised his boyhood *entheos* for God and Country games; and finally slicing the feared Franco-Spanish Armada and destroying the ensuing three digestible pieces at the battle of Trafalgar to earn the timeless Caesarean accolade, *'Veni, Vidi, Vici'* aka 'I came, I saw, I conquered'.

d. *Code 4 ~ Reading:* This is my beloved Ode to Mrs Chelvan, 'Reading maketh a full man'. Reading was the best of my schoolday's class lesson.

Quadrant VI: Illustration 1
Jun's Self Portrait: Legendary!

Postscript Two: Jun, this is not self-serving, but I kept the letters my Dad wrote me when I was away for two years in snowy Boston. I treasure and squirrel them away as a store of inspiration then and now. When my memory wanders to times past like 75 years ago, his 'hologram' comes before me of the dauntingly dangerous 125-mile walk from Endau-Mersing in the north-eastern Johor war resettlement zone to the Singapore Island to check on his parents and younger siblings' well-being during the harsh Japanese Occupation. In context my hiking, 10 to 30 miles, is but a relative cake walk. As an aside and in retrospect, I began to understand how my Dad appreciated my 'inherited' penchant for hiking and how he quietly nudged me in my toughening hikes, badges and parallel informal leadership role in scouting during my high school and university days.

Moreover, the Mersing-Singapore trek exposed Dad to the vicissitudes of the all-powerful patrolling soldiers; and he walked back safely after doing what he could to aid their survival. Thankfully, survive they did.

Dad's always there for me.

Quadrant VI: Illustration 2
50-Year Hour-Glass: Young Scout Hiking SG @ 1mph '58 & Malaysian Jungle @ 3mph '66

Quadrant VI: Illustration 3
YY & Jun: Buggy on Course

The year was 1958 in junior high school. I qualified for my first 'nervous-angst' public Radio/TV KLM World Travel "Magic Carpet" Quiz. My ever-knowing Dad as companion and coach gave me enormous confidence. I defeated the 'nervous-angst' as it became for me not about winning a twin-ticket trip with my Dad but I was inspired by him and his encyclopaedic knowledge of our world.

What gave me a hidden edge was my early 'mind's eye visualisation' and focus on what I would savour from the flying 'Magic Carpet', over the high snow-capped plateaus of old Persia on which sit Teheran, the Dutch windmills, dykes and tulips of Holland, London's Big Ben and Buckingham Castle to the highest buildings of the world across the Atlantic in New York. It, as though, aided me to 'spot' and anticipate the range of questions! As insurance, I chewed on every morsel of the ruling internet of those times – *The Encyclopaedia Britannica!* As my dear pal Philip Wee recalled to this day without fail, I notched an almost perfect 5/5, save for a disputed height of the Empire State Building (as some psychic recompense, it was the starting point as per the illustration for the 3,000-mile drive to San Francisco with Leo, a decade later). My Dad and I were sanguine, as the audience was with me on the 1,250 feet architectural height whereas the compere without a second thought pressed the buzzer for 1,350 adding100 feet for the Radio/TV antenna. This humbling lesson stood me in good stead when dealing with the complex stakeholder interests, years down the road in the eventually successful Chingay'09 and NTU-YOG'10 Village projects when at times some important interests possess a mix of being judge, jury and arbiter. *Jun, you need to be flexible. You may need to stand firm on your ground, if necessary.* So we did and stood our ground in about 1980. I had aided my fellow junior partners to assert our legal rights to a share of common property which I led in the purchase and financing. We cooperatively financed and retained wise legal counsels including Queens Counsel (three in fact) leading to a final mutual settlement and sweet conclusion for everyone, after about four years. It was equivalent to 3,000 economy tickets of 1958!

Three years later in 1961, my Dad accompanied me to the Istana for the 'joint-pride' of my young life – Queen Scout Conferment. Surreal but true, firstly it got me selected as National Patrol Leader for the Singapore Contingent to the 4th Thailand Scouts' Jamboree in Bangkok; and by sheer serendipity President Ishak recalled Dad giving him a civil defence evacuation ride at about Arab Street one February day in 1942 when bombs rained on our beloved island; and thence the Elders were deeply engrossed about the horrors of the war and the promise of a new generation. I was like the fly on the wall to witness oral history and the joie de la vie!

By coincidence, I met his brother, Minister of State Rahim Ishak, at the UN in New York and shared this episode. Upon his return, Rahim and Isteri Makwan so generously paid my Dad an unannounced visit and met our Miss Singapore Sister, Mag! As my younger brother Soon Kim recounted, the entourage with police outriders surprised our neighbours and gave my family a 'red-faced' five minutes of fame.

And the refrain from the *Sound of Music's* resounding ditty strikes a chord that:

> Nothing comes from nothing
>
> Nothing ever could
>
> So somewhere in my youth or childhood
>
> I must have done something good.

My gratitude to the notion that I did!

This I know, the confluence (or the 'Revenge of the Empire State Building') of all these did change and enrich my life through an osmotic transformation of reality and virtual-ity beyond imagination upon meeting the quintessential mythical-hybrid Jackalope in Wyoming, a thousand miles before San Francisco.

Cumulatively, the combo of Hong Kong and Singapore evokes in me so much in common with the Empire State's centre, New York City. So, it did aid me when doing business and operating in all three centres living and working in two spells each in NYC and HK; and home base in SG.

They were the bustling centres of finance, corporate and political power, enterprise, performing arts and sports, international-ity (versus region-ality), philanthropy, publishing and the physicality of epic sagas from Delano Roosevelt to Donald Trump (vis-à-vis our incomparable Tung Chee Hwa and Lee Kuan Yew.)

My Mom was not given to writing, but I have had dear, dear conversations and her unconditional love. I fondly recall the early morning countless birthday boiled-eggs with a dash of red for good luck in rock sugar syrup for a smooth life and the Australian IXL-brand marmalade which stood inspirationally sounding like *I Excel*. In a pensive mood my inner eye lights up to reflect on how blest I've been. How blest we have all been – sisters, brothers, our sons and daughters and you our Beloved Grandchildren!

Postscript Three: *Giant Mentors* My Scout Cub Mistress aka Akela imparted the early full lessons of hunting and caring for the pack. I learned self-sustaining enthusiasm to lead by force of authority and earned respect to survive and thrive in the green (and concrete) jungle. Such learning was reinforced by my Scout Master who became the Chief Commissioner and concurrently my Form Master and Shakespearean literature teacher Mr Leslie Woodford aka Black Bear, and by my devoted Rover Scout Master Henry Schooling aka Lone Wolf (as the to-be-obeyed wise, Alpha Matriarch Akela is also known). The scholar extraordinary young Law Dean Dr Tommy Koh who shaped and concluded the herculean global United Nations Convention on the Law of the Sea (UNCLOS) and a repertoire of the needed 21st century 30 Free Trade Agreements. He so kindly advised me on creating the symphonic collection on 'what Harvard means to alumna/us'. Now known as *The Crimson Essays* including MM (on his fellowship of 1968), George Yeo, Justice Andrew Ang, KL's Former Cabinet Secretary Tun Sarji, Beijing's COSCO Chairman Captain Wei, swimmingly shaped out by his early submission of how he chose Harvard Law School in his exemplary essay 'Letter from Dean Griswold', assisted the volume to completion in 9 months to July 2005. The collection of essays pleasingly raised $250,000 to top the targeted $1 million in endowing an alumni social enterprise for capacity building focused on board and CEO governance.

Postscript Four: *The Future's Arriving* – As I laid this letter to simmer in the back of my mind, I took ten days off. The surprise came when I went with Edmund Yong and visited his beloved and idyllic Queenstown in NZ South Island almost a stone's throw to Antarctica! Remarkably, the pioneers together with the founding Māori preserved their world and environment for their future generations. They have recently exceeded themselves by making River Whanganui a Legal Person and part of the society and community. What a novel thought. Besides adding to it our personal sense of water spirits I learnt 'beliefs of Shamans' from my co-hiker Dyak Mike trekking in the Perak jungles in 1966 through backwoods, streams and rivers. This will augment your reading of Greek mythology attesting to the mighty warrior Achilles, born of water Nymph Thetis and Peleus.

Interestingly, it seems a circular way. The future meets the past and forward, past meets the future! 'Zeitzeuge'. Germans say it another way that we cannot ignore history as it 'has a lasting hold **on** the present'. That's the uncanny feeling atop Cheyenne'69 vis-à-vis my boyscout night-hike guided only by the same North Star of the Big Dipper in a reverse southern-mirror night-sky over Kampung Buangkok'58 to our destination 5 kilometres away – Singapore's Coney Island. Toledo Ohio the first stop after 600 miles straight from New York City on my 50-year ago 3,000-mile drive across America has made Lake Erie a Legal Person, too. At 8,900 miles apart, from NZ to the USA, the same revolutionary decision was made (by creating) the future of Rivers and Lakes being Legal Persons at about the same time in 2019. But in truth they came from two different ends – the Whanganui River is in pristine settings whereas Toledo's nearby Cuyahoga River coursing into Lake Erie is probably one of the most densely polluted waterbodies which caught fire in 1969 (they instead set to save the Lake!) Any legal case precedents arising from these two cases might help in the fast developing Artificial Intelligence (AI) sector should the AI creators of 'Mr Data' of *Star Trek* seek to establish him to be a Legal Person.

Unthinkably, one day in your time, Jun, if an island nation like Iceland decides to make the island of Iceland a Legal Person, what would the other 44 island countries do then?

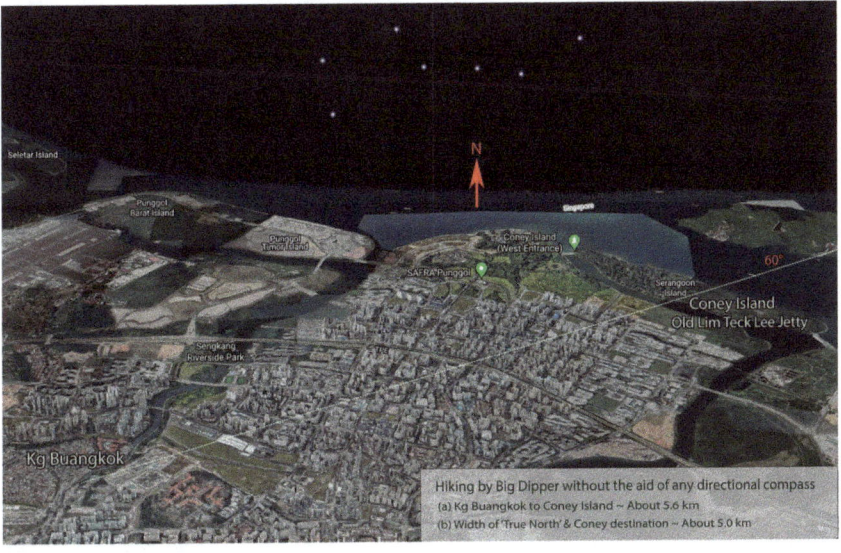

Quadrant VI: Illustration 4
1 NorthStar 2 Views: SG'58 & USA'69

Postscript Five: *Warning 2019* Where have all the birds gone? The first passing of the dinosaurs happened at the time of an extra-terrestrial explosion in the Gulf of Mexico creating the long winters that wiped them out. The second passing seems to be a prelude to the glaring loss of the successor hybrid dinosaurs – our beloved bird, fewer in numbers, less in body weight in a man-made climate and expanding human habitation change. The 2019 temperature at Alaska's Anchorage was 90*F which has risen from 75*F in 1969 at the time we were riding into San Francisco from water-stressed and arid Utah and Nevada! It's not a question of if, but when, the expected heat wave past 100*F will arrive. It may not be too far away.

Off the Dessert Menu ~ To top it all off, Jun, you can capitalise on your interest in Greek mythology by looking up Proteus as he and the Jackalope can transform into many shapes!

Quadrant VI: Sweet Conclusion   **117**

WARREN MCFARLAN
ALBERT H. GORDON PROFESSOR OF BUSINESS ADMINISTRATION EMERITUS

May 6, 2019

Mr. Anthony Teo
Email: anthonyteosc@suss.edu.sg

Dear Anthony,

It was such a pleasure to see you at the "Frontiers of Change" event this last weekend, and have the opportunity to get caught up over lunch. You not only came from farther away than anyone else, but you have also been involved with our Social Enterprise activity for a longer period of time than all but a tiny few in the room. We are so grateful that you made the effort to come from so far away.

We deeply value the four people per year that come to SPNM from Singapore each year. They add important global context to our case discussions.

I look forward to seeing you on campus soon again.

Cordially,

F. Warren McFarlan

FWM;mpd

P.S. It was fun reminiscing about our first program on Sentosa Island'81. Both my daughter and I remember the event with a great deal of fondness. It is hard to believe the barracks are now a casino.

Attachment I - Emailed Letter from HBS Professor Warren McFarlan on my provost-ship of HBS Global Forum on PRC & Post-WTO at Shanghai 2004 ~ 'From Sentosa AMP'81 to Shanghai'04, we both rose to the challenge'; and 25th Anniversary of embedding social enterprise in the MBA Programme at HBS 2019 ~ Few amongst the invited guests have engaged as long as you in the past 25 years ~.

Posted by Andy Tan, 15 Jan 2011

NTU's contributions to YOG Computed in Monetary Value

(A) Residential Halls and Student Volunteers

(1) Hostel rooms and facilities in UG Halls = $26,859,600.00
YOG (1 June to 29 Aug) – 90 days

	Units	Per day rate (with air-con)	Rental
Hall Rooms	5949	@$40 per pax	$ 21,416,400.00
Spare HF	8	@$150 per unit	$ 108,000.00
Common rooms	10	@$5928 average per hall	$ 5,335,200.00
Total			$ 26,859,600.00

(2) Sports facilities = $184,920.00
Assumption: Preferential rates for NSA used and based on a 12 hour day.

Facility	Computation	12 hr /day
Main Complex	$700	700.00
2 Multipurpose Field	12hrx2Fx$20	480.00
3 Basketball Courts	10hx3x$5 2hx3x$10	210.00
6 Tennis Courts	10hx6x$5 2hx6x$7	384.00
Sports Hall 1	10hX$35 2hx$40	430.00
Sports Hall 2/3	10hx$120 2hx$140	1480.00
3 Activity Rooms	12hrx3x$30	1080.00
Swimming Pool	$600	600.00
Floodlights	4hr X $200	800.00
		6164.00

Sports Facilities Cost per day $6164.00
If we assume the cost is for period of games plus setup, we can assume 30days x $6164.00, Total cost is $184,920.00

(3) Volunteers' manhours = $913,900.00
1406 volunteers
Average 5 hours per day
Only take YOG period (work done before the Games is not taken into the calculation) which is 14 to 26 August
Assuming that volunteers are paid, the applicable and reasonable hourly rate is $10.
Calculation: 1406 x 5 hours x 13 days x $10 = $913,900

Attachment II (1/5) - $100 million inherited assets in return for estimated 1.5-year $30 million of incremental sweat and guile; NTU-YOG Village hands-on Deputy Andy Tan, 15 January 2011.

(4) Hostel rooms in PG Hall and volunteers' manhours = $444,560.00
   (a) Revenue loss from rental:

   No. of Single Rooms: 364 at $380/month, $12.30/day

   No. Twin-Sharing / Spouse Rooms: 58 at $540/month, $17.40/day

   Period of YOG (from handing till taking over of GH): 2 months 19 days (11 June 10 – 29 August 10)

   Revenue Loss: 364 [(380x2) + (12.30x19)] + 58 [(540x2) + (17.40x19)]
   $= 361710 + 81820$
   $= \underline{\$443,530}$

   (b) Manpower (Student buddies' assistance for relocation efforts after YOG):

   Number of student buddies engaged : 16 at $8 / hr
   Number of man hours: 8

   Manpower expenditure: 16x8x8
   $= \underline{\$1,030}$

The value of services and facilities contributed towards YOG under this section is **$28,402,980.00**.

(B) YOUNG REPORTERS AND VILLAGE DAILY

60 students produced the newsletter, and for academic work we pay $7/hour for student helpers
14 days @ 10 hours per day (production)
14 days @ 5 hours per day (preparation)
14 days x 15 hours x 60 students x $7/hour = $88,200.

Printing the daily YOV newsletter was around $25,000

Extra costs (such as transport) were around $10,000

Staff costs (not on NTU payroll) were around $40,000

The total cost under this section is **$163,200**.

(C) OTHER COSTS

Venue	Charges for the first 2 hours	Per hour charge	Hours subjected to per hour charge	Per Day Charges	Days	Per Month Charges
LT1	300	180	12	2460	30	73800
LT2	250	96	12	1402	30	42060
LT3	120	72	12	984	30	29520
LT4	120	72	12	984	30	29520
LT5	120	72	12	984	30	29520
LT6	120	72	12	984	30	29520
LT7	250	96	12	1402	30	42060
LT8	250	96	12	1402	30	42060
LT9	120	72	12	984	30	29520
LT10	120	72	12	984	30	29520
LT11	120	72	12	984	30	29520
LT12	250	96	12	1402	30	42060
				$ 14,956.00		$ 448,680.00
TR1	70	35	12	490	30	14700
TR2	70	35	12	490	30	14700
TR3	70	35	12	490	30	14700
TR4	70	35	12	490	30	14700
TR5A	70	35	12	490	30	14700
TR5	40	20	12	280	30	8400
TR6	40	20	12	280	30	8400
TR8	40	20	12	280	30	8400
TR9	40	20	12	280	30	8400
TR11	70	35	12	490	30	14700
TR12	70	35	12	490	30	14700
TR13	40	20	12	280	30	8400
TR14	40	20	12	280	30	8400
TR16	40	20	12	280	30	8400
TR17	40	20	12	280	30	8400
TR19	70	35	12	490	30	14700
TR20	70	35	12	490	30	14700
TR21	70	35	12	490	30	14700

Attachment II (3/5)

TR22	70	35	12	490	30	14700
TR23	70	35	12	490	30	14700
TR24	70	35	12	490	30	14700
TR25	70	35	12	490	30	14700
TR25A	70	35	12	490	30	14700
TR26	70	35	12	490	30	14700
TR27	70	35	12	490	30	14700
TR27A	70	35	12	490	30	14700
TR28	70	35	12	490	30	14700
TR29	70	35	12	490	30	14700
TR30	70	35	12	490	30	14700
TR31	70	35	12	490	30	14700
TR32	70	35	12	490	30	14700
TR33	70	35	12	490	30	14700
TR34	70	35	12	490	30	14700
TR35	70	35	12	490	30	14700
TR36	70	35	12	490	30	14700
TR37	70	35	12	490	30	14700
TR38	70	35	12	490	30	14700
TR39	70	35	12	490	30	14700
TR40	70	35	12	490	30	14700
TR41	70	35	12	490	30	14700
TR42	70	35	12	490	30	14700
NIE3-B1-17 (Tutorial Room)	50	25	12	350	30	10500
NIE3-B1-22 (Tutorial Room)	80	40	12	560	30	16800
NIE3-02-03 (Tutorial Room)	70	35	12	490	30	14700
TR43	70	35	12	490	30	14700
TR43A	150	75	12	1050	30	31500
TR44	70	35	12	490	30	14700
TR45	70	35	12	490	30	14700
TR46	70	35	12	490	30	14700
TR47	50	25	12	350	30	10500
TR48	50	25	12	350	30	10500
TR49	50	25	12	350	30	10500
TR50	50	25	12	350	30	10500
TR573	40	20	12	280	30	8400
TR574	40	20	12	280	30	8400
TR51	50	25	12	350	30	10500
TR52	50	25	12	350	30	10500

Attachment II (4/5)

TR53	50	25	12	350	30	10500
TR54	50	25	12	350	30	10500
TR55	50	25	12	350	30	10500
TR56	50	25	12	350	30	10500
TR57	50	25	12	350	30	10500
TR57A	70	35	12	490	30	14700
TR58	50	25	12	350	30	10500
TR59	50	25	12	350	30	10500
TR60	50	25	12	350	30	10500
TR61	50	25	12	350	30	10500
TR61A	70	35	12	490	30	14700
TR62	50	25	12	350	30	10500
TR63	50	25	12	350	30	10500
TR63A	70	35	12	490	30	14700
TR64	50	25	12	350	30	10500
TR65	50	25	12	350	30	10500
TR66	50	25	12	350	30	10500
TR69	50	25	12	350	30	10500
TR71	50	25	12	350	30	10500
TR72	50	25	12	350	30	10500
				$ 32,900.00		$ 987,000.00
				Grand Total		$ 1,435,680.00

Attachment II (5/5)

Quadrant VI: Sweet Conclusion

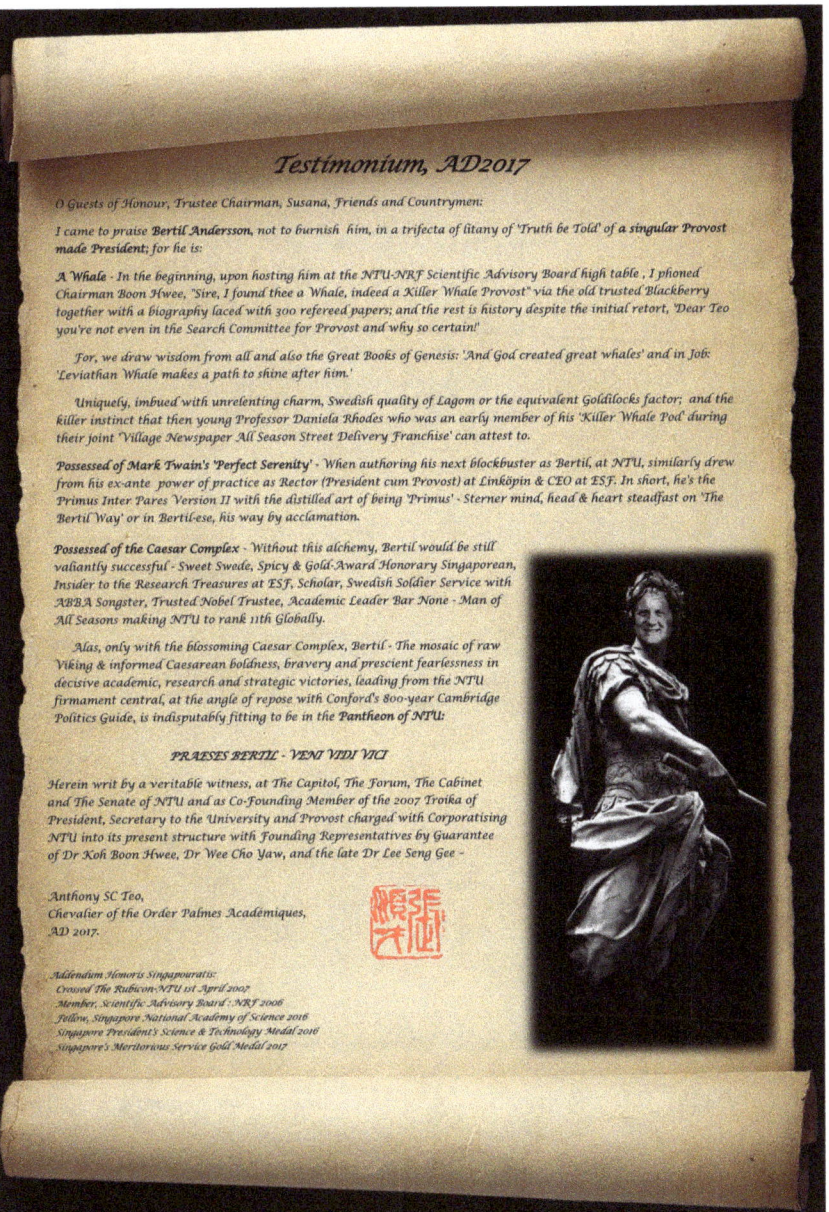

Testimonium, AD2017

O Guests of Honour, Trustee Chairman, Susana, Friends and Countrymen:

I came to praise **Bertil Andersson**, not to burnish him, in a trifecta of litany of 'Truth be Told' of **a singular Provost made President**; for he is:

A Whale - In the beginning, upon hosting him at the NTU-NRF Scientific Advisory Board high table, I phoned Chairman Boon Hwee, "Sire, I found thee a Whale, indeed a Killer Whale Provost" via the old trusted Blackberry together with a biography laced with 300 refereed papers; and the rest is history despite the initial retort, 'Dear Teo you're not even in the Search Committee for Provost and why so certain!'

For, we draw wisdom from all and also the Great Books of Genesis: 'And God created great whales' and in Job: 'Leviathan Whale makes a path to shine after him.'

Uniquely, imbued with unrelenting charm, Swedish quality of Lagom or the equivalent Goldilocks factor; and the killer instinct that then young Professor Daniela Rhodes who was an early member of his 'Killer Whale Pod' during their joint 'Village Newspaper All Season Street Delivery Franchise' can attest to.

Possessed of Mark Twain's 'Perfect Serenity' - When authoring his next blockbuster as Bertil, at NTU, similarly drew from his ex-ante power of practice as Rector (President cum Provost) at Linköpin & CEO at ESF. In short, he's the Primus Inter Pares Version II with the distilled art of being 'Primus' - Sterner mind, head & heart steadfast on 'The Bertil Way' or in Bertil-ese, his way by acclamation.

Possessed of the Caesar Complex - Without this alchemy, Bertil would be still valiantly successful - Sweet Swede, Spicy & Gold-Award Honorary Singaporean, Insider to the Research Treasures at ESF, Scholar, Swedish Soldier Service with ABBA Songster, Trusted Nobel Trustee, Academic Leader Bar None - Man of All Seasons making NTU to rank 11th Globally.

Alas, only with the blossoming Caesar Complex, Bertil - The mosaic of raw Viking & informed Caesarean boldness, bravery and prescient fearlessness in decisive academic, research and strategic victories, leading from the NTU firmament central, at the angle of repose with Conford's 800-year Cambridge Politics Guide, is indisputably fitting to be in the **Pantheon of NTU**:

PRAESES BERTIL - VENI VIDI VICI

Herein writ by a veritable witness, at The Capitol, The Forum, The Cabinet and The Senate of NTU and as Co-Founding Member of the 2007 Troika of President, Secretary to the University and Provost charged with Corporatising NTU into its present structure with Founding Representatives by Guarantee of Dr Koh Boon Hwee, Dr Wee Cho Yaw, and the late Dr Lee Seng Gee -

Anthony SC Teo,
Chevalier of the Order Palmes Académiques,
AD 2017.

Addendum Honoris Singapouratis:
Crossed The Rubicon-NTU 1st April 2007
Member, Scientific Advisory Board : NRF 2006
Fellow, Singapore National Academy of Science 2016
Singapore President's Science & Technology Medal 2016
Singapore's Meritorious Service Gold Medal 2017

Attachment III - *Testimonium 2017 on how NTU became Top 11th Globally.*

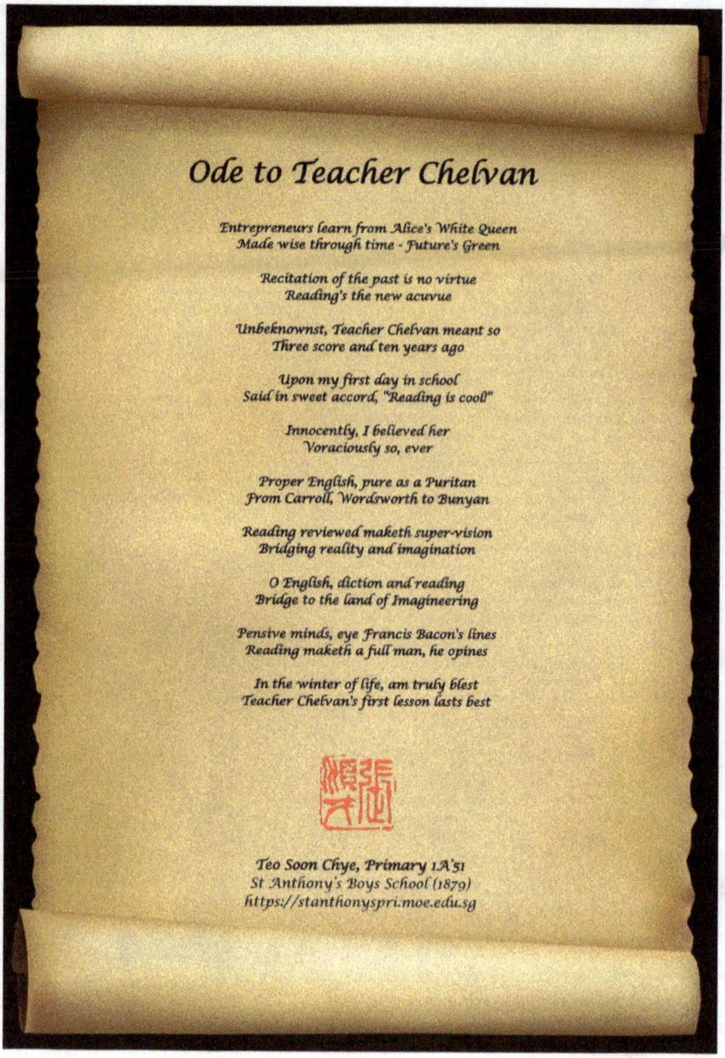

Ode to Teacher Chelvan

Entrepreneurs learn from Alice's White Queen
Made wise through time - Future's Green

Recitation of the past is no virtue
Reading's the new acuvue

Unbeknownst, Teacher Chelvan meant so
Three score and ten years ago

Upon my first day in school
Said in sweet accord, "Reading is cool"

Innocently, I believed her
Voraciously so, ever

Proper English, pure as a Puritan
From Carroll, Wordsworth to Bunyan

Reading reviewed maketh super-vision
Bridging reality and imagination

O English, diction and reading
Bridge to the land of Imagineering

Pensive minds, eye Francis Bacon's lines
Reading maketh a full man, he opines

In the winter of life, am truly blest
Teacher Chelvan's first lesson lasts best

Teo Soon Chye, Primary 1.A'51
St Anthony's Boys School (1879)
https://stanthonyspri.moe.edu.sg

Attachment IV - *Ode to Primary One Teacher Mrs Chelvan ~ 'Reading maketh a full man'.*

www.ingramcontent.com/pod-product-compliance
Lightning Source LLC
Chambersburg PA
CBHW071006160426
43193CB00012B/1934